# MONTEREY'S
◆ ◆ ◆
# SECRETS

◆

*Whispered Recipes and Guide to Inns, Restaurants
and Wineries of the Monterey Peninsula.*

◆

by Kathleen DeVanna Fish
with Fred Hernandez

◆

The Marketing Arm – Monterey, California

Library of Congress Cataloguing-in-Publication Data

Monterey's Secrets

Whispered Recipes and Guide to Inns, Restaurants and Wineries of the Monterey Peninsula

Fish, Kathleen DeVanna
88-090799
ISBN 0-9620472-0-1
Includes index page 236
Autobiography page 239

Copyright 1988 by Kathleen DeVanna Fish

Photography by Robert N. Fish
Cover photo at Ventana
Drawings by James Ogle on pages 9, 11, 61, 101
Cover design by Jerry Takigawa Design
Monterey Peninsula map by Wendy Crockett
Wine map compliments of the Monterey Wine Country Associates
Type by Metro Typography


Published by The Marketing Arm
P.O. Box 1994
Monterey, California 93942

Printed in the United States of America

# CONTENTS

## Enchanting Inns

# Distinctive Dining

## Monterey County's Extraordinary Wineries

## Monterey County
## North To South

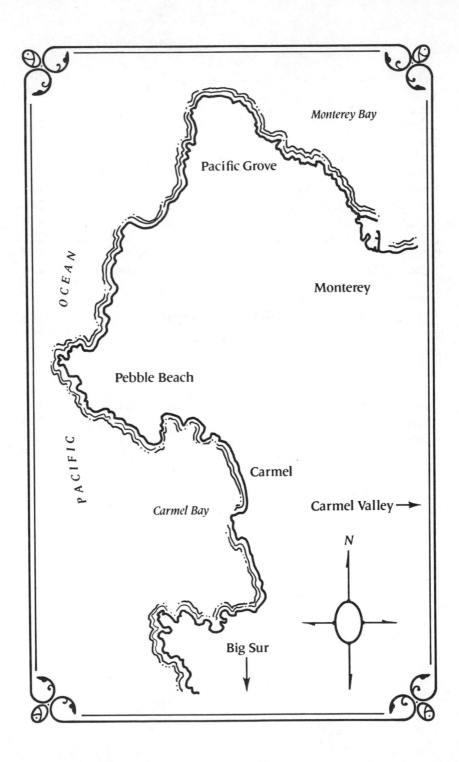

Monterey Bay

Pacific Grove

OCEAN

Monterey

Pebble Beach

PACIFIC

Carmel

Carmel Bay

Carmel Valley →

N

Big Sur

FALLING IN LOVE with the Monterey Peninsula is easy to do, especially if you know the secret hideaways.

That's what this book is all about: secrets.

Included are recommendations for unforgettable places to stay—inns with walled gardens and sunset views from Victorian parlors, inns where the visitor enters another world.

Then there is the incomparable food of the Monterey Peninsula. The bulk of this book is about exquisite food. Selections include treasured recipes from the inns and wineries. The restaurants go one step further: they provide full menus and their closely-guarded recipes.

SAVOR SUCH DELICACIES as crab saffron bisque, warm escargot salad, salmon mousse Wellington, P'ad Thai prawns, medallions of veal with pistachio butter sauce, vegetable terrine with cognac or chocolate decadence. Or how about some goat cheese fritters with apricot sauce or roasted garlic you spread like butter.

To make life easy, the book is divided into six geographical zones, from north to south: Monterey, Pacific Grove, Pebble Beach, Carmel, Carmel Valley and Big Sur. Recommended inns and restaurants—and their recipes—are listed for each zone.

Wineries you should know about are listed in a separate section. The wineries offer exceptional ways to cook with wine.

AND, TO HELP YOU get into the spirit of romance and adventure, each zone is introduced with tidbits of history, legend and lore. You'll learn about a lovely walled garden where grizzly bears and bulls fought to the death, about a submarine attack, smugglers, and movie stars dressed up for polo matches.

You'll discover where to enjoy a picnic while watching whales swim by, about sea lions that balance on rocks and look like modern sculptures, butterflies that cover tree branches, the town where blue laws outlawed liquor until 1969, and the real location of Treasure Island.

Discover the magical experience that lies hidden on the Monterey Peninsula. You'll never look at it the same way again.

# MONTEREY: THE ROMANTIC HUB

THE FIRST TOURIST visited Monterey in 1602, when Sebastiano Vizcaino of Spain sailed into Monterey Bay. And the visitors have just kept coming to the romantic hub of the Monterey Peninsula.

By 1770, six years before the Declaration of Independence was signed, Monterey was declared the capital of Alta California. That makes Monterey older than the United States.

Since that time, the city has survived pirates, naval attacks, bandits, duels in the streets, tales of sea serpents, and suitors serenading their sweethearts in secluded patios.

AND THROUGH it all, Monterey has carefully nurtured a reputation for fine cooking. The availability of a wide variety of fresh seafood and easy access to fertile fields and vineyards insure that the tradition is maintained.

Wander through the jumble of downtown streets and you will understand that the streets were set up to follow meandering cowpaths. And, like the twisting cowpaths, Monterey's history is mixed with legend, mystery and charm.

FOR EXAMPLE, the Memory Garden, a walled yard at the Pacific House is a tranquil spot to sit and enjoy the old fountain's water lilies and well-tended flowers. But this was also the spot where an early California form of entertainment took place. Grizzly bears and bulls, each with a leg tied to a single rope, fought to the death to the cheers of the crowd.

California's First Theater, dating from 1847, still offers theatrical productions. The first show packed the 150-seat house at $5 per ticket. You'll recognize the theater—it's the one with whale ribs on the front porch.

The Old Whaling Station, built in 1847, is a lovely two-story house with manicured gardens. At one time, it was headquarters for a company of Portuguese whalers, complete with a front walk made of whalebone. Next door is the first brick building erected in California. The owner left Monterey as soon as gold was discovered in the Sierras.

THE FIRST constitution of California was signed in 1849 in Colton Hall. The hall, now a museum adjacent to the city's municipal center, houses memorabilia of that historic time. In counterpoint to the origins of Colton Hall, a redwood tree in front of the graceful edifice was grown from seeds that were carried to the moon by astronauts.

9

MANY OF the graceful adobe structures of the old days are preserved to this day. Many are still in use, others are preserved as historic monuments and are open to tours.

Cannery Row was immortalized by author John Steinbeck. The sardine canneries have been converted to other uses or have been torn down. But some of the places featured in his books still remain: Doc Ricketts' Lab is a private club; Lee Chong's grocery store now sells souvenirs, and the Hovden Cannery has been completely rebuilt to house the Monterey Bay Aquarium.

A wealth of salmon and sardines formed the backbone of Monterey's economy for much of this century. In 1918, there were nine canneries along the waterfront. By 1945, there were 19 canneries operating full-bore. In some years 230,000 tons of sardines were canned or reduced for fish meal and oil.

In 1945, the sardines began to disappear. By 1950, what had been the greatest sardine port in the world was virtually a ghost port in the fishing industry. The rusting remains served as a setting for some of Steinbeck's most famous novels.

SOME OF THE history and lore of those hectic days is preserved at the Monterey Bay Aquarium, a $50 million facility that specializes in the critters of Monterey Bay and their habitats. One of the few aquariums that specializes in indigenous critters, the huge facility houses thousands of specimens.

Attractions at the aquarium include a sea otter tank complete with private beach for the playful mammals, bat rays you can pet, a trout stream, a user-friendly tide pool, and a unique kelp forest in the world's tallest tank.

Fisherman's Wharf is the descendant of a series of Monterey wharves dating back to 1845. Accompanied by an ever-present chorus of barking sea lions, visitors browse through specialty shops, seafood markets and restaurants and catch rides on tour boats when the whales migrate past the Monterey shore. A nearby wharf, built in 1925, serves as a cargo pier and contains facilities for the commercial fishing industry.

MONTEREY DATEBOOK: Monterey Film Festival, February; Adobe Tour, April; Squid Festival, May; Monterey Triple Crown, at Laguna Seca Raceway, May; Merienda (Monterey's birthday party), June; The Blues Festival, June; Monterey National Horse Show, July; Obon Festival, July; Santa Rosalia Festival (blessing of the fleet), September; Monterey Jazz Festival, September; California Wine Festival, November; Posada Procession and Piñata Party, December.

11

# THE JABBERWOCK

598 Laine Street
Monterey, CA 93940
(408)372-4777

THE JABBERWOCK BED and Breakfast, a 7 room post-Victorian home, is only 4 blocks above Cannery Row and the Monterey Bay Aquarium. It's hidden behind an ivy wall in a quiet neighborhood. And when you pass through, you've entered Alice's Wonderland, finding ½-acre estate gardens with waterfalls overlooking Monterey Bay.

With spacious public areas and enclosed sunporch where you enjoy an array of hors d'oeuvres and sherry each evening, you can relax looking at the sailboats. Each room is appointed with antique or period furniture, down pillows and comforters and before bedtime, cookies and milk await you.

Every morning you awake to the fresh aroma of a full exciting breakfast. And when you have to leave, you will truly know that you have passed "Through the Looking Glass!"

The
Jabberwock

# Caviar and Stuff

*Preparation Time: 5 Minutes*

½ lb. cream cheese room temperature
½ small onion finely chopped
1 small jar red caviar (1¾ oz. jar)
2-3 teaspoons cream

Soften the cream cheese in a mixer, adding cream and onions. Gently fold in caviar. Serve with watercrackers.

# Artichokes and Stuff

*Preparation Time: 15 Minutes*

1 can artichokes, drained
1 cup sour cream
½ teaspoon beef bouillon crystals
2 tablespoons sesame seed oil
¼ cup chopped fresh dill

Quarter the artichokes and set aside. Combine last four ingredients and let stand at least 10 minutes for bouillon to dissolve. Fold in artichokes. Serve with crackers.

# OLD MONTEREY INN

500 Martin Street
Monterey, CA 93940
(408)375-8284

AN ARCHITECTURAL GEM in a forest-like setting, the Old Monterey Inn is a charming English country house with a unique sense of history and romance. The handsome half-timbered house sits on an oak-studded hillside in a quiet residential neighborhood, surrounded by more than an acre of beautifully landscaped gardens.

All 10 delightful rooms have private baths, and most feature wood-burning fireplaces, skylights and stained-glass windows. Each room is individually designed to be a romantic delight.

Complimentary breakfast, decanted sherry, fresh flowers and fruit, plus afternoon wine and cheese create a unique experience for the discriminating guest.

# Scones

*Preparation Time: 45 Minutes*
*Pre-heat oven to 350°*
*Yields: 15 scones*

| | |
|---|---|
| 3 cups white flour | 2 eggs |
| 4 teaspoons baking powder | ½ pint whipping cream |
| Dash of salt | ¾ cup raisins or currants |
| ½ cube butter, cut into 4 pieces | |

In a food processor blend flour, baking powder, salt and butter. Transfer the mixture into a large bowl and blend eggs, whipping cream and raisins. (If dough is too dry to hold together, add a little water).

Gently roll the dough into a ball and place on a floured surface. Roll to ¾ inch thickness. Use a 2-inch cookie cutter and cut into 15 scones. Save ¼ cup egg and cream mixture, add a little sugar and brush tops. Bake at 350°, 20-30 minutes.

Serve with butter and jam.

# Fruit Soup

*Preparation Time: 25 Minutes*
*Serves 8*

| | |
|---|---|
| ½ cup coarse-cut seeded watermelon | 1 cup cranberry juice |
| ½ cup strawberries | ½ cup orange juice |
| ½ cup coarse-cut peaches | ½ cup lemon or lime juice |
| 1 cup bananas | ½ cup wine or champagne (optional) |
| 1 cup apple juice | Fresh mint leaves |

Combine the first 9 ingredients in a blender, to make your stock. Add the following cut fruit: ½ cup each, strawberry halves, watermelon chunks, seedless grapes, peach slices, pineapple chunks, cantaloupe balls and honeydew balls.

The soup can be served at room temperature or cold. Flavors improve the longer the soup sits.

# BEAU THAI RESTAURANT

807 Cannery Row
Monterey, CA 93940
(408)373-8811

WALKING DOWN Cannery Row toward the aquarium, one gets the feeling of a street full of secrets. One enters a converted cannery, past shops and another restaurant, and climbs a flight of stairs.

Walk through a golden door at the top of the stairs and you will enter a discreet restaurant that caters mostly to locals. Everyone who discovers the Beau Thai is enchanted by the low-key atmosphere and marvelous food. Even the policy toward smokers is intriguing: if you use an outside smoker's bench, the house will buy you a glass of wine.

This is David Walton's Beau Thai Restaurant. Your eyes are delighted by rich colors, candles and fresh red roses. The diverse menu includes vegetarian dishes along with selections of beef, pork, fowl and seafood.

Please feel at home, relax and enjoy yourself.

> ## Chef Kouit Busadee's Menu for Four
> *Tomkati K'A Kai*
> *(Spicy Chicken Coconut Soup)*
> *Mee Grob*
> *(Crispy Noodles with Pork and Bean Sprouts)*
> *P'ad Thai*

# Tomkati K'A Kai

*Preparation Time: 15 Minutes*

**3 cups water**
**5 slices galanga root**
**1 cup coconut milk**
**1 cup straw mushrooms**
**2 cups chicken, cut into bite-sized pieces**
**3 tablespoons lemon juice**
**4 tablespoons fish sauce**
**1 stalk lemon grass, sliced**
**1 tablespoon chili paste**
**3 cayenne chiles**

In a sauce pan, combine the water, galanga root, lemon grass and mushrooms bringing the mixture to a boil. Add the chicken, coconut milk, lemon juice, fish sauce, and chile paste.

Cook approximately 10 minutes before adding ground chile to taste.

# Mee Grob

*Preparation Time: 10 Minutes*

½ lb. rice Vermicelli Noodles
½ cup pork, sliced in thin strips
 2 cloves garlic, crushed
 3 tablespoons vinegar
 2 tablespoons fish sauce
 2 tablespoons tomato sauce
 2 tablespoons sugar
 2 tablespoons shallots
¼ cup bean sprouts
 2 tablespoons carrots, shredded
 3 stalks green onion
 4 tablespoons vegetable cooking oil

To cook the noodles, use a saucepan or wok. Heat with enough oil to fry the noodles. Wait until the oil is very hot, then put the noodles in the wok, turn over very fast, take out, and set aside to drain.

Heat a saucepan with cooking oil, add the garlic and cook until brown. Add the pork, sugar, vinegar, fish sauce, and tomato sauce. Reduce the heat, until sauce is very thick. Take the sauce off the burner, and mix in the noodles.

Serve with shallots, chopped green onions, bean sprouts and shredded carrots on the top.

# P'ad Thai

*Preparation Time: 15 Minutes*

½ lb. Chantaboon rice noodles
½ package hard tofu
 8 shrimp or prawns
 2 garlic cloves
 2 eggs
 4 tablespoons fish sauce
 5 tablespoons sugar
 2 tablespoons tomato sauce
 4 tablespoons vinegar
 1 carrot, shredded
 1 cup bean sprouts
 2 stalks green onions
 3 tablespoons ground roasted peanuts
    Lemon slices
 4 tablespoons vegetable oil

   Soak noodles in warm water for 20 minutes. Remove from water and let drain.
   Lightly brown the garlic, shrimp and tofu in oil. Cook briefly. Add the egg and stir until cooked. Add the noodles, sugar, fish sauce, vinegar, and tomato sauce.
   Top with bean sprouts, shredded carrots, peanuts and lemon slice.

# DELFINO RESTAURANT

400 Cannery Row
Monterey, CA 93940
(408)646-1700

DELFINO'S OFFERS OCEAN-SIDE seating in the beautiful Monterey Plaza Hotel on the bay. The ambience conveys old-world elegance surrounded by light walnut woods, leather chairs and fine linens. The menu is Northern Italian cuisine of the Emilia-Romagna region. The food is as superior as the service, and all is graced by the dramatic ocean views. Reservations are advised.

The Monterey Plaza offers 290 deluxe rooms and 20 grand suites—most with sunset-facing patios and balconies. All the luxuries and conveniences are ready and waiting, plus a caring staff trained to provide a memorable hospitality experience.

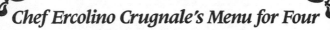

*Chef Ercolino Crugnale's Menu for Four*

*Salmon in a Fresh Basil Sauce*
*Tenderloin of Veal in Vodka Cream Sauce*
*Tomato Fusilli with Fresh Basil*

# Salmon in a Fresh Basil Sauce

*Preparation Time: 15 Minutes*

  4 salmon fillets, 8 oz. each
1½ oz. fish stock
  3 oz. butter
  2 oz. white wine
  2 oz. dry vermouth
  8 tomatoes, peeled, seeded and chopped
  1 oz. fresh basil, julienned
1½ oz. Pernod
    Salt and pepper to taste

Cook the salmon with the fish stock and ½ oz. butter in a saute pan. When the fish is cooked, remove from pan and place on a serving dish. Add white wine, vermouth, tomatoes, basil, Pernod and remaining 2½ oz. butter to the fish stock.

Spoon over the salmon and serve.

# Tenderloin of Veal
# In Vodka Cream Sauce

*Preparation Time: 30 Minutes*
*Pre-heat oven to 350°*

**2½ lbs. trimmed veal tenderloin**
**5 oz. thinly sliced pancetta**
**Salt and pepper to taste**
**2 tablespoons oil**

Season veal tenderloins with salt and pepper; wrap with pancetta and tie with butcher string. Brown the wrapped veal tenderloins in a hot pan with 2 tablespoons oil. Finish in a 350° oven for 12 minutes. The veal should be cooked medium. Let sit for 2 minutes, then slice and serve with Vodka Cream Sauce.

# Vodka Cream Sauce

**¼ lb veal, chopped coarse**
**1 tablespoon butter**
**1 teaspoon peppercorns**
**1 bay leaf**
**½ cup vodka**
**2 cups cream**
**2 cups reduced veal stock**
**¼ cup shallots, chopped**

Melt the butter in a saucepan, adding chopped veal with peppercorns, shallots and bay leaf. Saute the veal in butter until browned. Drain the butter. Add the vodka and flame it, to burn off alcohol. Add the cream and veal stock and reduce by one third or until sauce coats the back of a spoon.

Pass the sauce through a fine strainer and season with salt and pepper.

# Tomato Fusilli with Fresh Basil

1 lb. tomato fusilli
8 tomatoes, peeled, seeded and diced
2 tablespoons minced basil
2 cloves garlic, minced
4 oz. olive oil
  Salt and white pepper to taste.

Sauté the tomatoes, garlic and ¾ of basil with the olive oil in a sauté pan for about 2 minutes. Boil the fusilli and add them in the sauté pan. Bring to a boil and season with salt and pepper.

Separate the fusilli in soup plates. Garnish with the remaining basil and serve immediately.

# DOMENICO'S ON THE WHARF RESTAURANT

50 Fisherman's Wharf
Monterey, CA 93940
(408)372-3655

DOMENICO'S IS AN elegant, lively and eclectic seafood restaurant on Fisherman's Wharf, specializing in Italian cuisine.

While waiting for a table it's fun to mingle with the lively crowd at the oyster bar and sip a glass of wine from the large cellar of imported and domestic wines.

For dining with a view, tables are set along the windows the length of the dining room. Guests enjoy a never-ending water show of strutting sea gulls, diving pelicans, cavorting harbor seals and an occasional sea otter with his catch of the day, all set against the backdrop of Monterey's historic harbor and fishing fleet.

*Chef Nate Udomsri's Menu for Four*

*Tomato-Ginger Soup*
*Marinated Scallops*
*Seafood Pasta*
*Cannoli*

# Tomato-Ginger Soup

*Preparation Time: 45 Minutes*

2½ oz. ginger, peeled and sliced
 1 medium onion coarsely chopped
 2 lbs. plum tomatoes, peeled, seeded, chopped
 4 tablespoons unsalted butter
1¼ cups chicken stock
 1 tablespoon sugar
  Salt and pepper to taste
¾ cup cream
 2 egg yolks
  Watercress leaves for garnish

In a food processor, puree the onion and ginger until smooth. Transfer the mixture to a bowl. Add the tomatoes to the food processor, puree until smooth; set aside.

Melt the butter over medium heat in a large heavy saucepan. Add the onion puree and cook, stirring frequently, until the mixture begins to color, about 5 minutes. Add the tomato puree, chicken stock, sugar, salt and pepper. Bring the mixture to a boil, stirring occasionally. Add the cream, reduce the heat to low and simmer uncovered for 30 minutes. Taste the soup and add more sugar if necessary, to balance the acidity of the tomatoes.

Beat the egg yolks with a whisk to blend. Add the mixture to the saucepan and stir over medium-low heat until the soup thickens, about 2 minutes. Do not allow the soup to boil. Strain the soup through a fine sieve into a clean saucepan. If the soup is to sit any length of time, place a piece of plastic wrap directly against the surface to prevent a skin from forming.

Garnish with watercress leaves.

**25**

# Marinated Scallops

*Preparation Time: 15 Minutes (note refrigeration time)*

**1 lb. fresh scallops (20-30 count)**
**4 oz. water chestnuts sliced thin**
**1 leek diced (white part only)**
**5 mushrooms sliced**
**1 oz. shredded red ginger**
**1 tablespoon soy sauce**
**1 tablespoon honey**
**1 teaspoon rice vinegar**
**1 teaspoon sesame seed oil**
**1 tablespoon olive oil**
**Juice of ½ lime**
**1 garlic clove, minced**
**2 dashes of tabasco**
**Black pepper to taste**

Cook scallops in boiling, lightly salted water 5-7 minutes. Remove from heat, cool with cold water.

Mix the above ingredients together. Add the scallops. Marinade 2-3 hours before serving.

# Seafood Pasta

*Preparation Time: 20 Minutes*

**12 large shrimp**
**16 littleneck clams**
**16 mussels**
**16 shucked oysters**
 **8 oz. fresh scallops**
 **8 oz. squid**
 **5 garlic cloves, minced**
 **5 shallots, minced**
 **6 oz. butter**
 **4 cups marinara sauce**
 **4 oz. white wine**
**12 oz. clam juice**
   **Lemon and parsley garnish**
 **1 lb. cooked linguine**

   In a heavy sauce pot cook the shrimp lightly on both sides in butter. Add all ingredients except the squid. Cook for 5 minutes, then add squid and cover pot, until clams and mussels open.

   Serve over fresh linguine. Garnish with lemon crowns and sprinkle with chopped parsley.

27

# Cannoli Filling

*Preparation Time: ½ hour*

1 lb. ricotta cheese
  Grated rind of ½ orange
  Grated rind of ½ lime
4 oz. powdered sugar
2 oz. chocolate chips
2 oz. walnuts chopped

In a food processor blend ricotta cheese with powdered sugar for 3 minutes or until smooth. Transfer to a bowl, mixing the rest of the ingredients together. Refrigerate for 1 hour.

# Cannoli Shells

2 cups flour
2 teaspoons baking powder
2 teaspoons powdered sugar
2 tablespoons butter
1 egg
2 teaspoons vanilla
1 cup beer or wine
  Pinch of salt

Mix the above ingredients and knead into a ball. Cover, and allow dough to rest for one hour before rolling out and cutting to desired size. Deep fry until brown.

Stuff the cannoli filling into the shells and serve.

# THE FISHERY RESTAURANT

21 Soledad Drive
Monterey, CA 93940
(408)373-6200

THE FISHERY IS noted for its international cuisine and Asian specialties featuring a large selection of fresh seafood and a most extraordinary salad bar.

Owners Jerry Meyer and Glen Blanchar have traveled extensively throughout the Orient to sharpen their culinary skills and bring home many innovative recipes.

A cozy and inviting atmosphere where you can relax and enjoy your evening meal.

Mobil Travel Award winner.

*Chef Glen Blanchar's Menu for Four*

*Curried Squid Cocktail*
*Crispy Fish in Sweet and Sour Sauce*
*Nutcracker Flambé*

# Curried Squid Cocktail

*Preparation Time: 15 Minutes*

**2 lbs. squid fillets cleaned**
**6 tablespoons mayonnaise**
**1 tablespoon curry powder**
**1 cup green onions chopped**
**1 cup celery chopped**
**1 teaspoon salt**
   **Garnish with lettuce and tomatoes**

Dip squid fillets into rapidly boiling water. Cook for 2 minutes. Drain. Rinse with cold water and chop into bite-size pieces.

Mix together remaining ingredients and toss squid bits into mixture. Chill thoroughly.

Serve on a bed of finely chopped lettuce and chilled tomatoes.

# Crispy Fish in Sweet and Sour Sauce

*Preparation Time: 25 Minutes*

**Eight 10 oz. white fish fillets**
  **1 teaspoon garlic, chopped**
    **Oil for cooking**
  **2 tablespoons light soy sauce**
**¼ teaspoon salt**
**½ teaspoon sesame oil**
**¼ teaspoon ginger juice**
  **1 tablespoon water**
  **3 cups plus 2 tablespoons oil**
  **1 cup flour**
  **4 tablespoons cornstarch**
**1½ teaspoons baking powder**
    **Garnish with shredded lettuce**

Cut fish fillets into 1-inch cubes. Marinate in soy sauce, salt, sesame oil, ginger juice, water and 1 tablespoon oil, and let stand for 10 minutes.

Heat the wok and add 3 cups of oil. Combine the flour, cornstarch, baking powder and 1 tablespoon oil for batter. Add enough water to make the mixture runny. Dip the fish in the batter and deep fry in hot oil until golden brown. Drain and remove to a plate with slotted spoon and set aside.

Heat 1 teaspoon oil to stir fry garlic. Add sweet and sour sauce and bring to a boil.

To serve, garnish the fish cubes with shredded lettuce and serve sweet and sour sauce as dip.

# Sweet and Sour Sauce

Combine ¾ cup water, 3 tablespoons tomato sauce, 1 tablespoon tomato puree, 2 tablespoons vinegar, 3 tablespoons sugar, 1 tablespoon cornstarch, 1 chicken bouillon cube, ¼ teaspoon sesame oil and 1 teaspoon red chile. Mix well.

# Nutcracker Flambé

*Preparation Time: 5 Minutes*

**1 cup macadamia nuts, chopped**
**5 tablespoons butter**
**5 tablespoons brown sugar**
**1 oz. Amaretto**
**1 quart French vanilla ice cream**

Combine the nuts, butter and brown sugar in a saucepan over medium heat. Flambé with the Amaretto. Stir until the mixture is foamy and hot.

Pour over the ice cream until caramelized.

# FERRANTE'S RESTAURANT

The Monterey Sheraton
350 Calle Principal
Monterey, CA 93940
(408)649-4234

FOR THE BEST views on the Central Coast, Ferrante's offers an informal, creative Northern Italian restaurant high above the Monterey Sheraton. Spectacular 270-degree views of Monterey and the bay are experienced in a relaxing atmosphere. Exciting specialties, late night menu, elegant Sunday brunches and full bar make this restaurant a local favorite.

The Monterey Sheraton also includes 344 guest rooms, a fully equipped health club, sauna, hot tub, heated outdoor pool and Sheraton service second to none.

*Chef Bobby Stephens' Menu for Four*

Cream of Zucchini Soup
Stuffed Mushrooms
Fettucine Ferrante's

# Cream of Zucchini Soup

*Preparation Time: 25 Minutes*

5 medium zucchini
1 medium onion
1 quart chicken stock
¼ cup flour
¼ lb. butter
4 oz. cream
   Italian seasonings to taste
4 tablespoons parmesan cheese
6 sprigs of parsley chopped

Sauté the shredded zucchini and diced onions with butter until tender. Add the flour, chicken stock and seasoning. Stir and simmer until the soup is quite thick. Add the cream.

When serving, top with parmesan and parsley garnish.

# Stuffed Mushrooms

*Preparation Time: 15 Minutes*

12 large mushroom caps
 8 oz. prosciutto, julienned
 2 tablespoons dried oregano
16 oz. mozzarella, grated
 1 oz. parmesan, grated
 2 teaspoons garlic, pureed
 4 teaspoons parsley, chopped
   Black pepper to taste
   Lemon

Remove the mushroom stems and steam the caps (slightly crispy).

Mix all ingredients together in a medium mixing bowl, by hand. Making small balls from the mixture, stuff into cooked mushrooms caps.

Place the caps on a plate, in a circle, and top with a little parmesan cheese. Brown under the broiler.

Place on a lined plate and serve hot, with fresh lemon.

# Fettucine Ferrante's

*Preparation Time: 20 Minutes*

**28 oz. egg fettucine**
**4 cups chicken breast, julienned**
**1 head broccoli**
**1 cup cashews**
**1 cup parmesan**
**3 cups heavy cream**
**1 tablespoon garlic**
**Salt and pepper to taste**

Cook the egg fettucine al dente and set aside.

Sauté the chicken in a medium sauté pan to brown. Add the garlic, broccoli, seasonings and cream. Let the cream reduce on medium heat for 3 minutes. Add the cashews and fettucine.

Sprinkle with parmesan cheese before serving.

# FRESH CREAM RESTAURANT

100 F Heritage Harbor
Monterey, CA 93940
(408)375-9798

THE FRESH CREAM Restaurant creates an elegant mood, with a menu to match. This award-winning restaurant is noted for its distinctive French menu which changes nightly.

Chef-owner Robert Kincaid believes in using only the best available produce, meats and seafood.

Fresh Cream is a place for unhurried dining and quiet conversation in an intimate atmosphere.

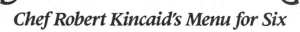

*Chef Robert Kincaid's Menu for Six*

*Saucisson de Veau en Croute*
*(Veal Sausage in Puff Pastry)*
*Salade d'espinard Vinaigrette de Sesame*
*Fillet de Salmon Grille Beurre Gingembre*

# Saucisson de Veau en Croute

*Preparation Time: 2½ hours*
*Pre-heat oven to 425 degrees*

½ lb. veal (30% fat)
½ lb. pork shoulder (30% fat)
4 oz. shallots
2 oz. garlic
1 tablespoon green peppercorns chopped
1 tablespoon parsley chopped
1 tablespoon basil chopped
¼ cup brandy
   Salt and pepper to taste
4 puff pastry dough sheets
   Egg wash

Grind veal, pork shoulder, shallots and garlic in a coarse grinder. Add the remaining ingredients and refrigerate for 2 hours.

Lay the sausage meat on the dough sheet and roll the ends. Place the sausage rolls on a baking sheet and brush the tops with egg wash.

Bake at 425° until brown (15-20 minutes).

Slice and serve.

# Salade d'espinard
# Vinaigrette de Sesame

2 tablespoons sliced chives
¼ cup rice wine vinegar
1 tablespoon sugar
2 tablespoons soy sauce
¼ cup salad oil
¼ cup sesame oil
2 bunches fresh spinach
   Sesame seeds

To make the vinaigrette, combine the vinegar, sugar, soy sauce and oils mixing well.

Toss the spinach leaves in the vinaigrette and garnish with toasted sesame seeds.

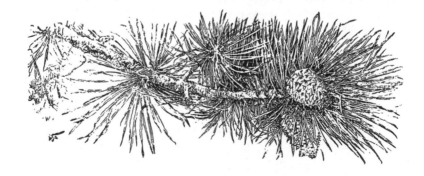

# Fillet de Salmon Grille Beurre Gingembre

*Preparation Time: 35 Minutes*

**Four 6 oz. salmon fillets**
**Juice from 2 oranges**
**Juice from 1 lemon**
**5 tablespoons soy sauce**
**1 teaspoon tomato puree**
**1 teaspoon garlic, chopped**
**3 tablespoons salad oil**
**1 tablespoon coriander**
**8 oz. butter**
**1 tablespoon chives**
**2 oz. ginger minced**
  **Salt and pepper to taste**
  **Garnish with lemon and parsley**

Combine the juice from the orange and the lemon, tomato puree, garlic, oil, coriander and 3 tablespoons soy sauce. Place the salmon fillets in the marinade and refrigerate for 30 minutes.

Mix the softened butter with chives, 2 tablespoons soy sauce, ginger, salt and pepper.

Grill or pan fry the salmon fillets to medium. Place the salmon on a baking sheet, putting 1 teaspoon of ginger butter on each fillet. Place under the broiler until the butter has melted.

Garnish the plates with lemon and parsley. Serve with vegetables, rice or potato.

# THE OLD HOUSE RESTAURANT

500 Hartnell Street
Monterey, CA 93940
(408)373-3737

THIS FAMOUS ADOBE, built in 1840, has been fully refurbished with an eye toward providing a setting reflecting the graciousness of California hospitality.

Like the art objects, antiques, furnishings and paintings you see about you here, The Old House's award-winning cuisine has been collected over many years and many miles of travel. Superb recipes encountered around the world have been adopted. Some dishes are purely original creations.

If the cuisine must be given a name, let it be called California-French.

*Chef Emile Labrousse's Menu for Four*

Halibut with Sorrel Buerre Blanc
Warm Escargot Salad
Chocolate Pecan Squares

# Halibut with Sorrel Buerre Blanc

*Preparation Time: 30 Minutes*

**24 oz. fresh halibut**
**½ lb. plus 1 tablespoon sweet butter, cubed**
**⅓ cup heavy cream**
**⅔ cup dry vermouth**
**⅓ cup shallots, chopped**
**3 cups fresh sorrel leaves, sliced thin**
   **Salt and pepper to taste**
**2 tablespoons safflower or grapeseed oil**

Sauté the shallots in a stainless pan with one tablespoon butter, stirring until limp. Add dry vermouth, reduce over low heat for 10 minutes. Add cream and sorrel. Remove the pan from the heat, and rapidly whisk in the cubes of butter. Reserve sauce in a warm spot, but do not boil.

Heat the oil in a non-stick frying pan. Sprinkle the halibut with salt. When the oil is very hot, fry the halibut for 10 seconds per side. Blot excess oil from fish.

Divide the Sorrel Buerre Blanc evenly among the four warm plates. Arrange the halibut on the sauce. Decorate each piece with a sorrel leaf.

# Warm Escargot Salad

*Preparation Time: 45 Minutes*
*Pre-heat oven to 350°*

5 dozen small escargot,
  cooked in Court Bouillon
  and strained
¾ lb. baby lettuce mix
  (arugula, red leaf, mache,
  etc.)
2 small red skin potatoes,
  cooked and cubed

3 garlic cloves, minced
3 oz. sweet butter
2 tablespoons parsley,
  chopped
1 tablespoon chives, minced
1 teaspoon thyme, minced
½ cup chicken broth

# Dressing

2 shallots, minced
1½ tablespoons balsamic
  vinegar

6 tablespoons virgin olive
  oil (cold press)
Salt and pepper to taste

# Garlic Toast

1 loaf French bread

1 whole head garlic

Cut the large lettuce leaves into bite-size pieces. Wash thoroughly, spin dry. Reserve in refrigerator.

Combine all the ingredients for dressing in a stainless bowl. Keep refrigerated until ready to use.

Slice the bread into thin slices on the diagonal. Brown in a 350° oven. Rub each piece with a clove of garlic, on one side only. Set aside.

Melt butter in a heavy skillet over high heat. When butter is foaming, add escargot and potatoes. After one minute add chicken broth, garlic, parsley, thyme, chives, salt and pepper. Simmer over low heat for three minutes.

Toss the greens with the dressing and arrange four toasts around the edge of each plate, garlic side up. Top each salad with the escargot mixture. Wilt the greens with the hot broth and serve the Escargot Salad without delay.

44

# Chocolate Pecan Squares

*Preparation Time: One hour*
*Pre-heat oven to 375 degrees*

3¾ cup flour
1½ tablespoons sugar
1⅔ cup butter
   2 eggs
   2 tablespoons milk
   2 tablespoons salt

   In a large bowl, combine all of the ingredients. Line a half sheet pan with sweet pastry. Prick dough evenly.
   Bake at 375° for 45 minutes.
   Cool before pouring the chocolate pecan mixture over the pastry.

# Chocolate Pecan Mixture

2½ lbs. pecans, roasted
   1 cup heavy cream
   ½ lb. sugar
1¼ lb. brown sugar
1½ bl. sweet butter
   1 lb. honey
   6 oz. semi-sweet chocolate

   Mix the above ingredients and pour over the sweet pastry.
   Cut into squares and serve.

# SARDINE FACTORY RESTAURANT

701 Wave Street
Monterey, CA 93940
(408)373-3775

THE SARDINE FACTORY, a popular and unique restaurant located at historic Cannery Row, is world renowned for its excellent cuisine, extensive wine list and impeccable service.

The cocktail lounge contains a 120-year-old hand-carved bar, and displayed on the walls is a pictorial history of Cannery Row. In addition to the original dining room, there are four other distinctive dining areas.

Ted Balestreri and Bert Cutino opened the Sardine Factory in 1968, and since that time have received numerous awards.

The Sardine Factory, with its warm and friendly atmosphere, superb service and excellent menu, offers the ultimate opportunity for elegant dining.

### Chef Dan Catanio's Menu for Ten

Crab Saffron Bisque
Salmon with Ginger Beurre Blanc
Hot Wilted Spinach Salad with Bacon & Mango Chutney Dressing
Lobster Wellington
Baked Polenta Parmesan
Grilled Zucchini, Bell Pepper and Olive Jumble
White Chocolate Mousse

# Crab Saffron Bisque

*Preparation Time: 1½ Hour*

| | |
|---|---|
| 4 lbs. fresh whole crabs | 2 bay leaves |
| 2 cups celery | 8 tablespoons sweet butter |
| 2 cups onions | ½ cup flour |
| 2 cups carrots | 2 cups cream |
| 2 cups leeks | 2 teaspoons saffron |
| 2 cups tomatoes diced | ½ cup sherry |
| 2 teaspoons peppercorns | Salt and white pepper to |
| 2 tablespoons thyme | taste |
| | 1 sheet puff pastry (optional) |

Cover the crab with water in a large soup pot and bring to a boil; skim off. Add onions, leeks, tomatoes, celery, carrots, thyme, bay leaves and peppercorn. Turn down to a simmer and cook for 30 minutes. Remove crab and crack shell for more flavor, then return to stock. Cook 30 minutes longer. Strain stock and reserve crab meat. Stock should yield eight cups. Add saffron.

Melt the butter in a small saucepan. Add the flour and cook over a low heat for 5 minutes. DO NOT BROWN. Add to your stock and cook over low heat for 15 minutes. Add one-half cup cream, salt, white pepper and sherry.

Whip the remaining cream until stiff. Cut and cook puff pastry into desired shape.

Pour soup into a bowl. Garnish top with crab meat, one spoon of whipped cream and puff pastry.

# Salmon with Ginger Beurre Blanc

**Ten 6 oz. salmon fillets**
   **Poaching Liquid—8 parts water to 1 part white vinegar**
 **3 oz. ginger root, crushed**
 **1 teaspoon shallots chopped**
**½ cup clam juice**
**½ cup chablis**
 **1 oz. mushrooms**
 **1 pint whipping cream**
**½ lb. sweet butter (cubed)**
**⅛ teaspoon white pepper**
**⅛ teaspoon salt**
   **Garnish with lemon twists, parsley sprigs and salmon caviar**

Cover salmon fillets with cold poaching liquid and cook over medium heat until simmer is reached. Remove from heat.

In a medium saucepan, add the ginger root and mushrooms. Add shallots, chablis and clam juice. Place over medium heat and reduce until almost dry. Add whipping cream and reduce to a third. Remove from heat, then add butter cubes slowly while constantly stirring. Strain sauce through a fine strainer.

Place fillet on a warm plate, lace with two ounces of the sauce. Place lemon twist and parsley sprig along the side. Top fillet with four or five eggs of salmon caviar.

# Hot Wilted Spinach Salad with Bacon and Mango Chutney Dressing

*Preparation Time: 20 Minutes*

6 bunches spinach leaves, cleaned and dry
1 lb. bacon, diced
½ cup shallots chopped
¼ cup white wine vinegar
6 oz. jar of Major Grey's Chutney
¼ cup white wine vinegar
½ cup olive oil
    Pinch of ground black pepper
    Chopped eggs (optional)

In a mixer, blend together chutney, vinegar and black pepper. Slowly add the olive oil.

In a large sauté pan, cook the bacon until crisp. Strain the bacon and keep the fat. In the sauté pan, add the bacon fat, shallots, vinegar and reduce by half. Add the chutney dressing to the pan and stir until hot. Take off the heat.

Add the spinach and toss until well coated and wilted. Divide onto plates and top with bacon and eggs.

This salad is also nice with fresh fruit.

# Lobster Wellington

*Preparation Time: 35 Minutes*
*Pre-heat oven to 375°*

**Ten 6 oz. lobster tail meat (Australian or South African)**
**7½ tablespoons sweet butter**
  **2 tablespoons shallots**
  **4 oz. brandy**
  **4 tablespoons olive oil**
  **2 sheets 4 × 4 filo dough**
  **4 tablespoons lemon butter**
    **Pinch of salt and pepper (white)**
  **2 teaspoons egg wash**
**1¾ cups heavy cream**
  **2 teaspoons paprika**

    Melt the butter and blend in the olive oil in a sauté pan. Add the shallots, lobster meat and 1 oz. brandy. Burn off. Let simmer until meat is ¾ done. Remove the lobster. Add the cream, paprika and seasonings to pan.

    Blend all the ingredients, adding the remaining brandy. Reduce. Wrap the lobster with lemon butter and filo dough and brush with egg wash.

    Bake in an oven for 20 minutes at 375° until pastry is light brown.

    Serve the sauce either on the side or over the Wellington.

# Baked Polenta with Parmesan

*Preparation Time: 45 Minutes (note refrigeration time)*
*Pre-heat oven to 400°*

**2 cups water**
**½ teaspoon salt**
**½ cup yellow cornmeal (not stone ground)**
**2 tablespoons unsalted butter**
**3 tablespoons freshly grated parmesan cheese**

In a heavy sauce pan, bring the water to a boil. Add the salt and the cornmeal in a very slow stream, whisking constantly. Cook the mixture over moderately low heat, stirring for 15 minutes, or until it is very thick. Stir in the butter and pepper to taste.

Spoon the polenta into a buttered 9-inch pie plate, and smooth the top. Sprinkle fresh parmesan over the top of the polenta.

Cover and chill the mixture for at least 30 minutes, or up to 12 hours.

Bake the polenta at 400° for 25 minutes. Brown it lightly on the rack of a pre-heated broiler, about 4 inches from the heat.

Cut it into wedges.

# Grilled Zucchini, Bell Pepper and Olive Jumble

*Preparation Time: 15 Minutes*

  **3** red bell peppers, cut into ½ inch pieces
  **3** tablespoons unsalted butter
**1½** lbs. zucchini, scrubbed, trimmed and halved lengthwise, and
       cut into ½ inch slices
  **16** kalamata olives, cut into strips
   **¼** cup pine nuts
       Opal basil or zucchini flowers for garnish

Cook the zucchini over the grill to make grill marks. Cut to portion size for six.

Sauté red pepper strips in butter until tender, add olives and stir occasionally for 5 minutes.

Place the zucchini on dinner plate and spoon pepper and olive mixture on each grilled zucchini. Top with chopped, roasted pine nuts.

Garnish plate with Opal basil or zucchini flowers.

# White Chocolate Mousse

*Preparation Time: 45 Minutes*

½ cup granulated sugar
½ lb. white chocolate (chopped into small pieces)
¼ quart milk
 1 tablespoon gelatin
¾ quart whipping cream (whipped until stiff)
 1 tablespoon water

Dissolve gelatin in cold water.

Mix the milk and sugar in a two-quart stainless steel pan, and put it on medium heat. When the milk boils, add the white chocolate. Keep stirring until the mixture starts to boil again. Remove from heat.

Transfer the mixture to a bowl, add the gelatin and mix in. Mix until cold (this process can be speeded up by putting the bowl on ice).

When the mixture is cold, fold in the whipping cream gently. Pour the mousse into ten clear glasses and refrigerate.

Top each with raspberry sauce to desired level.

# Raspberry Sauce

1 lb. raspberries
1 cup sugar

Gently mix raspberries and sugar. Keep overnight in a closed container. Beat mixture until pureed, then pass through a fine sieve.

# WHALING STATION INN RESTAURANT

763 Wave Street
Monterey, CA 93940
(408)373-3778

FAMED FOR ITS uncompromising quality of ingredients and for the originality of chef/owner John Pisto, the Whaling Station Inn is an extraordinary regional restaurant with a national reputation.

One block up from Cannery Row, The Whaling Station is a cozy, upscale haven where hearty conversation, great food and wine and expert service prevail. A secret place that local residents and business executives would prefer to keep to themselves.

The historic exterior of the restaurant hints at the traditional spirit to be found within. As you pass through the vine-covered entry into the large lounge, one senses the relaxing, intimate and elegant ambience.

# THE WHALING STATION INN
## RESTAURANT

## Chef John Pisto's Menu for Four

*The Fabulous Artichoke*
*Spicy Prawns*
*Pasta with Pancetta and Peas*
*Grilled Monterey Salmon with Salsa*
*Long Stemmed Strawberries with Grand Marnier and White Chocolate*

# The Fabulous Artichoke

*Preparation Time: One Hour*

**4 large artichokes**
**¼ cup mayonnaise**
**¼ cup vinaigrette**

Steam artichokes until you can pierce the bottom with a fork, approximately 45 minutes to one hour.

Open the artichoke like a lotus flower. Put a dab of mayonnaise on the heart and pour a vinaigrette over the entire artichoke.

Serve with crusty French bread. Enjoy!

# Spicy Prawns

*Preparation Time: 1½ Hours*

  16 large prawns
   1 tablespoon ground coriander
   4 chiles (2 chopped fine, 2 cut into strips)
   1 teaspoon salt
   1 teaspoon fish sauce
1½ cup vegetable oil
   6 sprigs coriander

Peel and devein the prawns, leaving the shell on the tail only. Rinse prawns with cold water and pat dry with paper towels. Rub the prawns with ground coriander, chopped chiles, salt and a little oil. Let stand for one hour.

Reserve the marinade. Heat the oil in a sauté pan, over medium high heat and sauté the prawns for 2 minutes on each side. Place prawns on a serving plate.

Using the remaining oil, stir into reserved marinade and bring to a quick boil. Add the fish sauce.

Pour over the prawns and garnish with sprigs of coriander and chile strips.

# Pasta with Pancetta and Peas

*Preparation Time: 45 Minutes*

½ lb. Italian dried pasta
1 cup pancetta (Italian bacon) cubed
½ cup onion chopped
3 garlic cloves
4 cups tomatoes chopped
1 cup baby peas
Salt and pepper to taste
½ cup grated romano cheese

Cook the pasta al dente.
Saute the pancetta, onions and garlic until brown. Add the tomatoes and peas. Season with salt and pepper.
Pour the sauce over the hot pasta. Sprinkle freshly-ground romano cheese over the sauce and serve.

# Grilled Monterey Salmon with Salsa

*Preparation Time: 45 Minutes*

**Four 8 oz. salmon steaks**
**¼ cup olive oil**
**2 tomatoes chopped**
**1 clove garlic**
**¼ cup chopped cilantro**
**Juice of 2 limes**
**Tabasco to taste**
**Salt and pepper**

Rub the salmon with olive oil, salt and pepper. Grill over a low flame, cooking slowly. Turn only once and remove when fish is opaque.

To make salsa, combine tomatoes, garlic and cilantro. Add the lime juice and season with Tabasco and salt and pepper to taste.

# Long-Stemmed Strawberries with Grand Marnier and White Chocolate

*Preparation Time: 25 Minutes (note refrigeration time)*

**16 long-stemmed strawberries**
**32 oz. white chocolate**
**8 oz. Grand Marnier**
 **Empty egg carton**
 **Hypodermic needle**

Rinse and clean the strawberries well.

Melt the white chocolate in a double boiler on medium heat. Dip half of each strawberry in the white chocolate and insert with the white chocolate side up, in empty egg carton to cool. Refrigerate for at least 1½ hours.

Prior to serving, inject each strawberry with ½ oz. of Grand Marnier.

# PACIFIC GROVE: NO LONGER BLUE

PACIFIC GROVE'S restrictive roots as a religious retreat were so pervasive that you couldn't buy a drink there until 1969. The liquor ban had been in effect for 96 years.

The grandeur of the Pacific Grove coast has always drawn visitors. Inland Indian tribes used to vacation there while seeking mussels, abalone, fish and tule elk. And, as early as the 17th century, Point Pinos was used as a landmark by Manila galleons on their way to Mexico.

But Pacific Grove (the locals call it P.G.) got its start in 1875, with the establishment of a Methodist summer retreat. The Methodists stayed in tents and, before long, began building Victorian homes right over their tents.

In contrast to the wild and woolly origins of other communities in the area, the pioneers of P.G. established a long list of restrictive blue laws. For instance, one blue law specified in detail the type of bathing suits that could be worn and other laws banned swimming, boating or fishing on Sundays. Only medicine could be sold on Sundays. Deeds to property banned all kinds of gambling, billiards, dancing, swearing and boisterous talk. Liquor could not be sold, bought or even given away.

A CURFEW BANNED anyone under age 18 from the streets after 8 p.m. in the winter and 9 p.m. in the summer. One law stipulated that all window shades had to be kept up until 10 p.m., so constables could peek in the windows, on the lookout for illicit hanky-panky.

ONE 1879 visitor, novelist Robert Louis Stevenson, had this to say about the Methodist retreat: "Thither, in the warm season, crowds came to enjoy a life of teetotalism, religion, and flirtation, which I am willing to think blameless and agreeable."

The final straw among the restrictions was the fence with locked gate that encircled the retreat. Designed to keep out undesirables, including peddlers from sinful Monterey, the locked gate and rigmarole required to get in and out led to a revolt.

In 1880, State Senator Benjamin Langford, tired of having to hike a mile to the retreat office to get the key to unlock the gate, took an axe to the gate. The gate was never replaced and nine years later, in 1889, the city was incorporated.

By 1880, lots in P.G. cost from $135 to $250. Furnished three-bedroom homes could be bought for $650.

A LOT OF THINGS have changed in Pacific Grove. But what hasn't changed is the spectacular location overlooking Monterey Bay and the Pacific Ocean, particularly when one travels on the five miles of scenic road that hugs the remarkable coast.

Take Ocean View Blvd. (try it on a bike) starting at the aquarium. Include a picnic lunch. You may see playful sea otters breaking shellfish on rocks they carry on their chests, sea lions perched atop rocks and looking like futuristic sculptures or squadrons of brown pelicans swooping low over the water in search of lunch.

THIS STRETCH of coast is one of the best places in the world to spot the massive grey whales that pass by on their annual migration from Alaska to Baja California, where they breed. The whales take a short break in their migration to take in the sights of Monterey Bay. The migration begins in November, but the best time to see them spouting and leaping is January. One of the best spots to see them from shore is Lovers Point.

Along the shore, you will pass spectacular bed and breakfast inns with inspiring views of the ever-changing bay, a pathway afire with the "magic carpet" of bright pink ice plant blossoms, and massive tide pools teeming with plant and animal life.

Fishing boats often congregate off the P.G. shore, even at night, when the squid boats work with bright lights upon the water.

LOVERS POINT, a favorite spot for outdoor weddings, is a great place to spread out a picnic blanket on the lawn or the beach and watch the surfers. The sheltered beach was blasted out with dynamite in 1904 by William Smith. With the rock he blasted loose, Smith also built the stone wall and pier that still stand. In the old days, glass-bottomed boats explored the kelp forest and its wealth of sea life. Today, scuba divers flock to the point's underwater wonderland.

Lovers Point is the site of the major events of the Feast of Lanterns, celebrated every July. Begun in 1905, the charming pageant recreates the much-altered legend of a wealthy Chinese mandarin who had a beautiful daughter, whom he called Queen Topaz. Promised in marriage to another wealthy mandarin, Topaz instead fell in love with a poor student and ran away with him. In the original story, based on the Blue Willow china pattern, the lovesick girl drowned herself rather than marry a man she didn't love. In the P.G. version, Topaz and the poor student depart in a burst of fireworks, as Monarch butterflies. But not to worry: they return for the pageant every year.

The Pacific Ocean and Monterey Bay converge at Point Pinos, the northern tip of the Monterey Peninsula. You may want to visit the lighthouse, built in 1855. But be careful on the road—the foghorn may startle you if it goes off.

FURTHER DOWN Sunset Drive, past the Great Tide Pool and the rolling sand dunes and partially hidden among the pine trees, stands the Asilomar Conference grounds. Early plans for the grounds and the structures were developed by Julia Morgan, architect of the Hearst Castle at San Simeon.

Architecture plays a large role in P.G. Many of the old homes have been preserved and restored. In wandering through town, you may notice small signs on some of the older homes. The signs indicate when the houses were built and the name of the original owner. Some of the mansions and larger homes have been converted into bed and breakfast inns. The Victorian Home Tour, part of the P.G. Good Old Days celebration in April, is a good opportunity to get inside a selection of the best buildings.

Another event worthy of note in P.G. is the annual Butterfly Parade, held every October. The parade gives the town's schoolchildren a chance to march through town in a colorful variety of costumes, mostly of Monarch butterflies.

GREAT FLOCKS of the orange and black butterflies arrive each year in October and November and spend the winter in P.G. Sometimes there are so many that they cover the branches and leaves of the "butterfly trees".

Visitors should note St. Mary's by-the-Sea Episcopal Church, the oldest church in town. Built in 1887, the beautiful wooden church boasts two exquisite Tiffany stained-glass windows.

Also worth a visit are the P.G. Museum of Natural History and nearby historic Chautauqua Hall, where Pacific Grove was born amid Methodist meetings and lectures.

PACIFIC GROVE DATEBOOK: Wildflower Show at P.G. Museum, April; P.G. Good Old Days, Quilt Show and Victorian Home Tour, also in April; Feast of Lanterns, July; Lovers Point Catamaran Race, September; Butterfly Parade, October; Christmas at the Inns, December.

# CENTRELLA HOTEL

612 Central Ave.
Pacific Grove, CA 93950
(408)372-3372

IT IS DAWN. Light filtered through lace curtains dances across your covers. From a nearby window, you feel the cool salt air. You pull the down-filled cover close to your chin and curl up for another few minutes of sleep. A bath in a claw-foot tub beckons you, however. The brass handles squeak as you fill the tub with warm water and empty the bath salts.

As you make your way through the Inn's lofty corridors and around the arched beams of the attic suites, you are reminded of a time long ago forgotten. This 19th century Victorian has a large, open parlor room that captures the charm of the era.

Laid out before you on a polished oak table is a sumptuous breakfast. An old waffle iron is just beginning to heat up and the scent of freshly ground coffee is pervasive. Whoever said you can never go back in time has never stayed at The Centrella.

# Ellen's Eggs & Sausage Sandwich

*Preparation Time: 15 Minutes*
*Serves 6*

  2 tablespoons butter
  2 tablespoons flour
  1 cup sour cream
12 eggs
  1 cup grated cheese

Melt butter, add the flour and cook briefly. Stir in the sour cream and cook until hot and bubbly. Meanwhile, crack the eggs and whip. Cook in a non-stick skillet over medium heat, stirring constantly. Add sour cream mixture just as eggs begin to solidify. Do not overcook. Turn off heat and stir in grated cheese.

# Sausage Sandwich

*Preparation Time: 45 Minutes*
*Serves 12*

  1 onion chopped
1½ lbs. breakfast sausage
  ½ cup parmesan cheese
  1 cup Swiss cheese, grated
  2 eggs, beaten
  ¼ teaspoon Tabasco
  ⅓ cups parsley, chopped
  3 cups biscuit mix
1½ cups milk
  ⅓ cup mayonnaise
    Egg wash

Sauté the onions and sausage. Drain the fat and cool slightly. Add cheeses, egg and Tabasco. Combine biscuit mix, parsley, milk and mayonnaise. Spread half of thick batter in 9" × 13" pan. Cover with sausage mixture and spread with remaining batter. Paint with egg wash. Bake 30 minutes at 375°.

# GOSBY HOUSE INN

643 Lighthouse Ave.
Pacific Grove, CA 93950
(408)375-1287
1-800-342-4888

UPON ENTERING THE Gosby House Inn you are greeted by the warm and hospitable staff. Fine appointments enrich the interior of the restored Victorian mansion that boasts a collection of rare antiques. An open-hearth fireplace entices visitors to gather and enjoy afternoon tea, sherry, fresh fruits and hors d'oeuvres. Each morning a delicious breakfast is tastefully prepared and served in the parlour or the garden patio.

The accommodations are inspired by the comfort and luxury of fine European country inns; each room reflects this mood with polished natural woods, soft comforters, delicately colored wallpapers and flowers. Fireplaces are available in some rooms, and most rooms have a private bath.

The Gosby House Inn is located in the heart of the historic seaside town of Pacific Grove, with its many Victorian homes and beautiful shoreline.

# Sour Cream Coffeecake

*Preparation Time: 1½ Hours*
*Pre-heat oven to 350°*
*Yield: 1 bundt pan—10"*

1 cup butter (2 sticks) softened
2¾ cups sugar
2 eggs, beaten
⅛ teaspoon salt
2 cups sour cream

2 cups white flour
1 tablespoon baking powder
1 tablespoon vanilla
2 cups pecans, chopped
2 tablespoons cinnamon

Grease and flour bundt pan. Cream the butter and 2 cups of the sugar. Add eggs, blend, add the sour cream and vanilla.

Sift together the flour, baking powder and salt. Fold the dry ingredients into the creamed mixture, and beat until just blended. Do not overbeat.

Mix together remaining ¾ cup sugar with pecans and cinnamon.

Pour half of the batter into the bundt pan. Sprinkle with half the pecan and sugar mixture. Add the remaining batter and top with the remaining pecan mixture.

Serve warm.

# Lemon Curd

*Preparation Time: 15 Minutes*

2 cups sugar
12 egg yolks, strained
1 cup lemon juice
½ lb. unsalted butter
2 tablespoons zest

Combine the sugar and egg yolks in a saucepan. Stir in the lemon juice gradually. Cook over low heat, stirring constantly until mixture coats the back of a spoon. Do not boil. Remove from heat, whisk until cooled. Stir in butter and zest. Cool. Store in refrigerator. Keeps for weeks.

# Chocolate Decadence

*Preparation Time: 25 Minutes (note refrigeration time)*
*Pre-heat oven to 425°*
*Serves 10*

**1 lb. semisweet chocolate**
**5 oz. butter**
**5 large eggs**
**1 tablespoon flour**
  **Whipping cream for garnish**

   Grease a 9" or 10" cake pan or souffle dish and line it with wax paper.
   Melt the chocolate and butter in a saucepan.
   Beat the eggs and flour in a separate bowl and set in a pan of hot water. Blend the chocolate mixture into the egg and flour mixture.
   Pour into the cake pan or souffle dish, and bake 15 minutes at 425°. Cover with foil and freeze after baking.
   Garnish with whipped cream.

# Steamed Chocolate Almond Pudding

*Preparation Time: 1½ Hours*

5 oz. semisweet chocolate
3 oz. unsweetened chocolate
½ cup plus 2 tablespoons butter, softened
⅔ cup sugar
6 egg yolks
⅔ cup finely ground toasted almonds
¼ teaspoon almond extract
8 egg whites
   Pinch of salt

Place both chocolates in a bowl. Set over barely simmering water. Stir until melted and smooth. Remove from the heat and cool.

In a mixing bowl, beat the butter and sugar until it is pale yellow and fluffy. Add the yolks and beat until very light, about two minutes. Fold in the almonds, extract and chocolate.

In a large bowl beat the egg whites and a pinch of salt until stiff peaks are formed when the beater is lifted. Fold into the chocolate mixture gently.

Place nuts on the bottom of a fluted pudding mold (8 cup). Spoon the batter into the mold, covering tightly. Add boiling water 1" up the side of the pudding mold.

Simmer gently 50-60 minutes or until a skewer inserted in the center comes out clean. Let cool 5 minutes before unmolding. Serve with whipped cream.

# GREEN GABLES INN

104 Fifth Street
Pacific Grove, CA 93950
(408)375-2095
1-800-841-5252

THIS ROMANTIC QUEEN Anne-styled mansion by-the-sea will capture your heart and imagination at first sight. A half-timbered, step-gabled residence, built in 1888, the Green Gables is an exquisite gem among Pacific Grove's many Victorian homes. Set on the edge of the Pacific shoreline, the Green Gables enjoys a spectacular panoramic view of Monterey Bay. The fairy-tale setting is further enhanced by the warm personal attention given to the guests.

The parlor features large bay window alcoves facing the bay, a lovely collection of antique furnishings and a unique fireplace framed by stained-glass panels.

In the afternoon, tea, sherry and wine are available in front of a cheery fire. In the morning, a delicious breakfast is served in the dining room with a panoramic view of the bay.

# Herbed Roulade

*Preparation Time: One Hour*
*Pre-heat oven to 350°*

   **2 tablespoons oil**
   **2 eggs**
   **½ cup flour**
   **1 cup milk**
   **2 teaspoons fresh chives**
   **1 tablespoon fresh parsley chopped**
   **2 teaspoons fresh dill**

   Brush a 11" × 17" jelly roll pan with oil.
   Beat the eggs for 15 seconds until pale yellow. With a mixer on, add the milk in a slow stream. Add the flour and mix until smooth. Add the herbs. Let the mixture rest for 30 minutes.
   Bake for 12 minutes at 350°. Cool in the pan and loosen the bottom with a metal spatula.

# Filling

**5-6 ripe avocados, chopped**
   **2 onions, chopped**
      **Butter for sautéing**
**1½ lbs. mushrooms, sliced**
   **½ lb. grated cheddar**

   Sauté onions and mushrooms. Mix all ingredients together. Spread filling over the entire crepe and roll lengthwise.
   Heat slightly when ready to slice.

# Vegetable Terrine with Cognac

*Preparation Time: 2 Hours*
*Yield: 5 cup loaf pan*
*Pre-heat oven to 350°*

## Carrot Layer

1½ cups sliced carrots plus
    4 julienned pieces
2 tablespoons butter
¾ teaspoon nutmeg
⅛ teaspoon allspice

½ teaspoon sugar
2 tablespoons heavy cream
1 tablespoon cognac
1 egg
1 egg yolk

## Broccoli Layer

2 cups fresh broccoli, plus
    extra for garnish
2 tablespoons heavy cream
2 tablespoons butter

½ teaspoon nutmeg
¼ teaspoon salt
1 egg

## Potato Layer

1½ cups potato chunks,
    peeled
1 cup onion, chopped
4 tablespoons butter
¼ cup heavy cream
1 tablespoon cognac

1 teaspoon curry powder
¼ teaspoon salt
    White pepper
1 egg
1 egg yolk

    Saute the carrots in butter over low heat until carrots are tender. Don't let carrots or butter brown! Add remaining ingredients for carrot layer. Using a food processor or blender, mix until blended. Set aside.

    Simmer broccoli in water until tender. Add remaining ingredients for broccoli layer. Process until blended. Set aside.

Saute the potato and onion in butter until potato pieces are tender and onion is soft. Don't let potatoes or onions brown! Process potatoes and onion until smooth. Add remaining ingredients for potato layer. Process until blended. Set aside.

Butter a 5 cup loaf pan and line it with wax paper. Cut another piece of wax paper to fit the top. Butter one side of the wax paper.

Pour carrot puree into bottom of pan. Smooth to make an even layer. Top with broccoli puree. Smooth. Top with potato puree. Smooth. Press buttered side of wax paper over potato layer. Place the terrine in a pan and add enough hot water to come halfway up the outside of the terrine. Place in a 350° oven and bake for 1½ hours or until a knife inserted into the center comes out clean. Allow to rest for 15 minutes in the oven with the heat turned off.

When terrine is cool enough to handle, remove the wax paper from the top. Invert the terrine and remove the remaining wax paper.

Garnish top with carrots and broccoli flowerets. Refrigerate. Serve cold.

# Spiced Whole Wheat Apple Bread

*Preparation Time: One hour*
*Pre-heat oven to 350°*
*Yields: 2 small loaves*

1½ cups flour
   1 cup whole wheat flour
   1 teaspoon salt
   1 teaspoon baking soda
   1 teaspoon baking powder
   2 teaspoons cinnamon
   ¼ teaspoon ginger
   ¼ teaspoon nutmeg
   3 tablespoons shortening
   ⅔ cup brown sugar
   2 eggs
   1 cup buttermilk
   ½ cup pecans
   2 apples, peeled and chopped

Combine the dry ingredients. Cream together the shortening, brown sugar and eggs. Add the buttermilk. Mix the dry ingredients with the liquid ingredients. Mix in the pecans and apples.

Divided the batter evenly between two loaf pans. Bake at 350° for 45-50 minutes.

# Tropical Banana Bread

*Preparation Time: 1½ hours (note elapsed time)*
*Pre-heat oven to 350°*
*Yields: One large loaf*

 1 cup currants
½ cup dark rum
 3 cups flour
 1 teaspoon salt
 1 teaspoon baking soda
 1 teaspoon baking powder
 2 teaspoons cinnamon
½ teaspoon nutmeg
½ cup coconut plus 2 tablespoons (for topping)
½ cup shortening
 1 cup brown sugar
 2 eggs
⅓ cup buttermilk
 1 cup mashed ripe bananas

In a small bowl steep the currants in heated rum for one hour.

Combine the dry ingredients. Mix the liquid ingredients. Stir together until just combined. Add the rum-soaked currants and pour into a loaf pan.

Sprinkle the top with 2 tablespoons coconut and bake at 350° for one hour.

# THE MARTINE INN

255 Oceanview Blvd.
Pacific Grove, CA 93950
(408)373-3388

TAKE A STEP BACK in time to gracious living with a complimentary breakfast served on Victorian china, Sheffield silver, crystal and lace.

This grand old home, built in the late 1890s, overlooks the magnificent rocky coastline of Pacific Grove.

Each of the 19 rooms has a private bath and is elegantly furnished with antiques. Many rooms have ocean views and wood-burning fireplaces.

Read in the library, sun-bathe in the landscaped enclosed courtyard, watch whales, sea otters, sailboat races or the fishing fleet from the two sitting rooms. Enjoy yourselves.

# Crab and Spinach Crepes

*Preparation Time: 20 Minutes*
*Makes 24 crepes*

## Crepes

¾ cup flour
2 teaspoons sugar
1 teaspoon salt
4 eggs
4 egg yolks
1 quart milk
1 tablespoon butter

Sift dry ingredients. Beat egg and milk until blended. Mix the egg mixture into the dry, blend until smooth.

Using clarified butter, cook over a medium heat, 2 tablespoons of batter per crepe, depending on the thickness desired for the crepes.

## Crab and Spinach Filling

1½ cups shredded crab
2 bunches spinach, chopped
Juice of one lemon
1 teaspoon dried thyme
1 teaspoon dried dill
Pepper to taste
1½ cups cream cheese

Mix all ingredients thoroughly and place 2 tablespoons of the crab mixture in each crepe.

# Salmon Mousse Wellington

*Preparation Time: 15 Minutes (note elapsed time)*
*Serves 4*

 1 cup flaked salmon
 2 green onions chopped
   Juice of one lemon
½ cup mayonnaise
 1 cup whipped cream
 1 package gelatin mix
 2 cups water—1 cold, 1 hot
   Dash of hot sauce
 1 sheet frozen puff pastry
   Egg wash

Mix the salmon, green onion, lemon, mayonnaise and hot sauce. In separate bowl combine the gelatin mix with one cup cold water until blended. Mix in hot water and blend all ingrdients together. Gently fold in the whipped cream. Refrigerate 4 hours or until set.

Cut the puff pastry into four equal pieces. Fill each pastry piece with ¼ to ½ cup salmon mousse filling. Fold long edges together and press with a fork to seal. Baste with egg wash.

The Salmon Wellington can be served with a hollandaise sauce.

# Oriental Chicken Salad

*Preparation Time: 25 Minutes (note elapsed time)*
*Serves 8*

5 lbs. chicken breast, cooked and cubed
1 cup raisins
2 cups celery, diced
1 cup walnuts, chopped
½ cup pimentos, diced
2 cups water chestnuts, sliced

# Dressing

½ quart peanut oil
3 oz. sesame oil
12 oz. rice wine vinegar
12 oz. water
2 oz. honey
2 oz. soy sauce
1 oz. lemon juice
3 garlic cloves, chopped
½ teaspoon salt
2 teaspoons black pepper
3 tablespoons ground ginger
1 tablespoon curry
2 oz. toasted sesame seeds.

Mix all ingredients for dressing.
Add chicken, raisins, celery, walnuts, pimentos and water chestnuts.
Marinate for 6-24 hours.

# Peanut Butter Vegetable Soup

*Preparation Time: 25 Minutes*
*Serves 6*

½ cup onion, chopped
1 large carrot, peeled and sliced
1 large stalk celery, chopped
2 garlic cloves, minced or pressed
1 tablespoon salad oil
1 cup chunk-style peanut butter
8 cups chicken broth
1 medium potato, scrubbed and diced
⅛ teaspoon cayenne
3 tablespoons red wine vinegar
   Salt and pepper to taste
   Chopped peanuts
   Garnish with parsley sprigs

In a 4 quart pan over medium heat, combine onion, carrot, celery and garlic with oil, stirring often, until onion is limp. Remove from heat and add peanut butter. Stir to blend with the vegetables. Stir in broth, adding potatoes and cayenne. Bring to a boil.

Reduce heat to simmer, cover and cook until potatoes are done, approximately 15 minutes. Add vinegar and salt and pepper to taste.

Garnish with peanuts and parsley.

# Lemon Cream Cheese Dessert

*Preparation Time: 15 Minutes*
*16 ½ oz. servings*

 1 cup milk
½ cup lemon juice
 1 lb. soft cream cheese
 1 cup sugar
 2 packages lemon Jello
 3 cups water

Blend the milk, lemon juice, cream cheese and sugar together. Gently fold in two packages of lemon Jello and water. Spoon into 16 ½ oz. sherbet cups or champagne glasses.

Let mixture set before adding Sour Lemon Topping.

# Sour Lemon Topping

½ cup lemon juice
½ cup water
½ cup sugar
 4 eggs

Blend together all ingredients. Over medium heat bring to a boil stirring constantly. When mixture has thickened, remove from heat and cool before spreading the topping.

# PACIFIC GROVE INN

581 Pine Ave.
Pacific Grove, CA 93950
(408) 375-2825

THE INN HAS 10 suites, decorated with the Queen Anne-style cherry furniture, matching fabrics and wallpapers and brass beds. Each guestroom has a gas fireplace, full bath and a small refrigerator. Some of the guest rooms have bay views.

The Pacific Grove Inn opened in May, 1986 after a year-long restoration of this magnificent Victorian, built in 1904. The house is now listed in the National Register of Historic Places.

# Crab and Three Cheese Strata

*Preparation Time: 45 Minutes (note elapsed time)*
*Pre-heat oven to 350°*
*Serves 12*

1 loaf sourdough bread, cubed
1 cup ricotta cheese
¼ lb. shredded Monterey Jack cheese
¼ lb. shredded sharp cheddar cheese
½ lb. Dungeness crab meat
2 tablespoons chopped green chiles
12 eggs slightly beaten
6 cups milk
5 tablespoons melted butter
¼ teaspoon dry mustard

Butter a 9″ × 14″ baking dish. Layer the bread with ricotta, crab, Jack and cheddar cheese and chiles.

Blend eggs, milk, butter and mustard in a large pouring bowl. Pour over bread mixture, covering all of it.

Cover the Strata with plastic wrap and refrigerate overnight.

Bake at 350° for 30 minutes or until eggs are set.

# SEVEN GABLES INN

555 Ocean View Blvd.
Pacific Grove, CA 93950
(408)372-4341

THE SEVEN GABLES Inn is a century-old Victorian mansion situated on the very edge of Monterey Bay. All guest rooms have panoramic ocean views and private baths. A very generous light breakfast is served in the formal dining room each morning. Four o'clock high tea is set out on the inviting sunporch featuring an unparallelled view of the bay and rocky coastline.

The furnishings throughout the Inn are formal Victorian and feature fine European, Oriental and American antiques. Intricate Persian carpets, crystal chandeliers, inlaid sideboards, beveled-glass armoires and gilt pier mirrors set an elegant atmosphere.

Owner-operated by the Flatley family, the Inn's atmosphere is one of careful attention to detail, friendliness and quiet hospitality reminiscent of an earlier time.

# Apple Harvest Muffins

*Preparation Time: 45 Minutes*
*Pre-heat oven to 325°*
*Yields 1½ dozen large muffins*

2¾ cups flour
 ¾ cup unprocessed bran
 1 cup sugar
 1 cup brown sugar (packed)
1½ tablespoons cinnamon
 3 teaspoons baking powder
1½ teaspoons salt
 1 teaspoon baking soda
1¼ cups oil
1½ teaspoons vanilla
 4 eggs
 3 ripe apples, peeled, cored and chopped

In a large bowl combine flour, bran, sugars, cinnamon, baking powder, salt and baking soda and mix very thoroughly. Add oil, vanilla, eggs and chopped apples. Mix just until blended.

Fill greased muffin tins ¾ full. Bake at 325° for 25-30 minutes or until brown.

Cool, remove from pan and serve warm with butter, favorite preserves or just plain.

# FANDANGO RESTAURANT

223 17th Street
Pacific Grove, CA 93950
(408)373-0588

FANDANGO BRINGS TOGETHER the flavors of the world's prized culinary regions. North African couscous... Spanish paella and tapas... Canneloni Nicoise... These are examples of the world of wonderful food the Fandango chef, Pedro De La Cruz, produces every day.

Whether your mood is carefree or quiet, social or private, Fandango has a dining area to suit you. Spend an intimate evening in the dining room, accented with fresh flowers and fireside dining. Celebrate a special occasion in the stonewalled wine cellar, privately tucked downstairs. Enjoy the perfumed aromas from the wood grill in the terrace room or soak up the sun on the outdoor patio. Enjoy!

*fandango*

**Chef Pedro De La Cruz's Menu for Six**

*Salade Nicoise*
*Paella A La Pierre*
*Creme Brulee*

# Salade Nicoise

*Preparation Time: 25 Minutes*

1 head butter lettuce or red lettuce, washed and drained.
2 medium tomatoes, quartered
⅓ green, red and yellow bell pepper, cut in ¼ inch strips
1 heart of celery, diced
½ cucumber, peeled and sliced
3 green onions, chopped
1 medium potato, boiled and diced in ½" cubes
1 cup cooked green string beans
1 cup canned tuna, drained (preferably water-packed)
6-12 anchovy fillets
½ cup Nicoise olives (packed in brine, not oil)
3 hard-boiled eggs, quartered
   Several fresh basil leaves, chopped
   Vinaigrette

Arrange lettuce around a salad bowl. Place tomato quarters on tops of lettuce leaves. Combine bell peppers, celery, cucumber, potatoes and green beans and arrange decoratively on top of tomatoes. Sprinkle the tuna and chopped basil on top of vegetables. Top each salad with 1 or 2 anchovy fillets, 2 egg quarters, a few olives and green onions.

Dress the salad with vinaigrette immediately before serving and toss lightly.

# Paella A La Pierre

*Preparation Time: 1½ Hours*

Olive oil
2 medium onions, chopped
2 cloves garlic, chopped
1 chorizo sausage (about ½ lb.) sliced ½ inch thick
1 large tomato, diced
3 tablespoons parsley, chopped
2 large pinches of saffron threads
3 cups chicken broth
1½ cups white rice (do not use minute or quick-cooking rice)

4 lbs. chicken, boned
½ lb. scallops
½ lb. calamari, sliced in 1-inch pieces
½ lb. shrimp, peeled with tails intact
6 littleneck clams
6 mussels
1 cup frozen peas
Fresh parsley for garnish

Set aside 1½ cups of chicken broth and soak saffron in remaining broth.

In a paella pan, very large skillet or wok, heat olive oil and cook onions and garlic until they are transparent. Add chorizo, parsley and all but 2 tablespoons of the tomato and cook until chorizo is browned. Add chicken and cook 5-10 minutes or until chicken is firm. Stir in rice and reserved chicken broth, cover and cook over low heat for 20 minutes.

After 20 minutes stir in calamari and remaining broth with saffron, cover again and cook another 20 minutes.

Now stir in scallops and shrimp, cover and cook 10 minutes.

Stir in mussels, clams, reserved tomato and frozen peas and cook just until shellfish open.

Garnish with fresh parsley and serve at once, in the pan.

# Creme Brulee

*Preparation Time: 20 Minutes (note elapsed time)*

    2 cups heavy cream
    1-inch piece of vanilla bean
    12 egg yolks
    ½ cup sugar
    ¼ cup powdered sugar
    Six 1" × 4" custard ramekins

Combine cream and vanilla bean in a medium saucepan and scald. Do not boil. Remove from heat.

In a separate bowl, beat egg yolks and slowly blend in the ½ cup of sugar. Adding slowly, pour the scalded cream into the egg and sugar mixture. Place combined ingredients in the top of a double boiler and stir over medium heat until the custard thickens on the back of a wooden spoon.

Pour into custard ramekins and cool to room temperature. Refrigerate until serving time.

When you are ready to serve, sprinkle the powdered sugar over the custards, making sure to cover the entire surface evenly. Glaze under broiler, or if available, with a hot round brulee iron, until the sugar turns medium to medium dark brown. Serve immediately.

# PASTA MIA RESTAURANT

481 Lighthouse Ave.
Pacific Grove, CA 93950
(408)375-7709

AS YOU CLIMB the steps of this quaint Victorian house, you will be treated to the aroma of fresh garlic and herbs. Venture through the doors to view the colorful variety of appealing antipastos displayed on the nearby table.

The extremely personable owner, Maureen Signorella, decided to open a trattoria, as opposed to a ristorante, upon returning from a two year stint in Italy. She wanted to create her own "bella Italia" here in Northern California.

That was seven years ago, and actually nothing has really changed for her, except that instead of cooking and eating with a few people, she does it for a 100 or so people.

The food is prepared fresh each day by chef Daniel Vitanza with either Maureen or sister Kathy at the door to greet you.

*pasta mia*

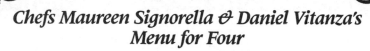

*Chefs Maureen Signorella & Daniel Vitanza's*
*Menu for Four*

Insalata Fresca
Pollo a'la Puttanesca Con Polenta
Zabaglione Freddo

# Insalata Fresca

*Preparation Time: 15 Minutes*

 2 pears
 1 large head radicchio
 ½ cup walnuts
 1 large fennel
 ¼ cup olive oil
    Salt and pepper to taste

   Wash radicchio and drain. Tear into bite-sized pieces.
   Quarter pears, core and cut crosswise. Add sliced fennel and walnuts.
   Toss with olive oil, salt and pepper to taste.
   Chill and serve.

# Pollo a'la Puttanesca Con Polenta

*Prepartion Time: 45 Minutes*
*Pre-heat oven to 350°*

     ½ tablespoon sliced garlic
     ½ cup calamata olives
      4 anchovies
     ½ teaspoon red chile pepper
      2 tablespoons capers
      3 cups tomato sauce
    2½ lbs. chicken pieces
     ¼ cup olive oil
      1 cup polenta, cooked

     Saute garlic, olives, anchovies, peppers and capers in 2 tablespoons olive oil. Add the tomato sauce and simmer for 2 minutes. Set aside.

     Pan fry the chicken pieces in remaining olive oil for approximately 15 minutes or until tender. Drain the oil and pat the chicken dry.

     Place chicken in a shallow baking pan and cover with the Puttanesca sauce. Cover the chicken and bake for 15 minutes at 350°. Serve the chicken and sauce over the polenta.

     This Puttanesca Sauce is also excellent over linguini.

# Zabaglione Freddo

*Preparation Time: 30 Minutes*

   8 egg yolks
   1 cup granulated sugar
½ cup Florio Dry Marsala Wine
   Orange zest
2 pints fresh berries
   Fresh mint leaves

   Mix the egg yolks, sugar, wine and orange zest in a double boiler. Begin whisking the ingredients, making sure the water underneath does not come to a full boil.

   The mixture will become light and fluffy in approximately 20 minutes. Zabaglione is cooked when mixture looks like whipped cream.

   Chill for approximately one hour.

   Pour over fresh berries in individual dishes and garnish with mint leaves.

   This zabaglione can be prepared the day before and refrigerated.

# PEPPERS MEXI CALI CAFE

170 Forest Ave.
Pacific Grove, CA 93950
(408)373-6892

WITHOUT A DOUBT, Peppers is one of the locals' most popular restaurants—and with good reason.

Specializing in Mexican and Latin American cuisine, Peppers takes the genre beyond the greasy tacos and refried beans. Peppers presents dishes that are fresh and simply prepared—with a great deal of imagination.

Seafood variations are featured daily and black beans offer a welcome change from the usual pinto beans. The traditional dishes are delicious; the innovative dishes are surprisingly good.

Peppers offers a warm, friendly atmosphere, an extensive wine list and an excellent selection of imported beers.

Open for lunch and dinner.

*Chef Scot Gonzalez's Menu for Four*

*Steamed Clams and Mussels with Mixed Bell Pepper Medley*
*Grilled Sea Scallop Salad with Cilantro Vinaigrette*
*Yucatan Prawns with Black Beans and Spanish Rice*
*Salsa Cruda and Avocado Salsa*

# Steamed Mussels and Clams with Mixed Bell Pepper Medley

*Preparation Time: 30 Minutes*

12 Littleneck or Manila clams
12 New Zealand mussels (may substitute East Coast mussels)
 1 Bermuda onion, sliced
 3 tomatoes diced
 1 red, yellow and green bell pepper sliced
 4 cloves garlic, sliced
 1 cup white wine
   Juice of 2 limes
 ½ stick butter
   Cilantro sprigs for garnish
   Tortillas

Clean and scrub mussels and clams. Use only the ones that are closed tightly.

Combine wine, lime juice and butter in a large sauce pan over medium heat. Add all vegetables and garlic and cook 3-5 minutes or until limp. Add clams and mussels, cover and simmer untill shells open. Discard any that don't open.

Pour into individual bowls and garnish with cilantro sprigs. Serve with warmed tortillas for dipping and scooping.

# Grilled Sea Scallop Salad with Cilantro Vinaigrette

*Preparation Time: 20 Minutes*

## Salad

1 lb. fresh sea scallops
1 each red lead, romaine and butter lettuce
3 sliced tomatoes
   Black olives, pitted
3 scallions

## Vinaigrette

2 tablespoons white wine
2 tablespoons orange juice
2 tablespoons fresh lime juice
2 tablespoons rice wine vinegar
6 tablespoons olive oil
½ cup chopped cilantro
   Pinch salt, sugar and pepper
1 clove garlic, minced

Combine all ingredients for the vinaigrette and mix well. Toss cleaned lettuce, torn into bite-sized pieces with the vinaigrette.

Grill or broil scallops until they are opaque in the center.

Garnish lettuce with tomatoes, olives, scallions and top with warm grilled scallops.

# Yucatan Prawns

*Preparation Time: 30 Minutes*

**2 lbs. medium-large prawns shelled, deveined and butterflied**
**1 red onion diced**
**.2 tomatoes diced**
**2 chiles diced**
**1 red bell pepper diced**
**¼ cup chopped cilantro**
    **Juice of 2 oranges**
    **Juice of 3 limes**
**¼ cup white wine**
**¼ cup fish stock**
**1 teaspoon oregano**
**½ teaspoon salt**

Combine all ingredients except the prawns in a large saucepan. Cook over medium heat for 10 minutes. Add the prawns and cook for 5 minutes.

Arrange prawns in individual bowls with portions of vegetables and broth. Garnish with chopped cilantro. Offer with Salsa Cruda or Avocado Salsa.

# Black Beans

*Preparation Time: 3 Hours*

**5 lbs. black beans**
**1 onion chopped**
**1 bell pepper chopped**
**3 cloves garlic chopped**
  **Bay leaf**
**3 tablespoons cumin**
**3 tablespoons chile pepper**

Sort beans for dirt and pebbles and wash well. Place in a large pot with all ingredients and cover with water. On high heat bring beans to a boil, reduce heat and cook until tender, about 2 hours. Add water as necessary to avoid drying out.

# Salsa Cruda

*Preparation Time: 5 Minutes*

**5 large tomatoes, chopped**
**1 onion**
**1 bunch of cilantro, chopped**
**2 serrano or jalapeño chiles**
  **Juice of one lime**

Mix the above ingredients for a zesty salsa.

# Spanish Rice

*Preparation Time: One Hour*

**2 cups long grain rice**
**2 tomatoes diced**
**1 cup tomato juice**
**1 onion diced**
**1 cup diced green chiles**
**1 tablespoon minced garlic**
**3 tablespoons olive oil**
**2 cups water**
**2 tablespoons salt**

Saute all vegetables in olive oil in a large sauce pan over medium heat. Add rice, water, tomato juice and bring to a boil, stirring continuously. Cover tightly and reduce heat to very low. Cook until done, approximately 30 minutes.

# Avocado Salsa

*Preparation Time: 5 Minutes*

**5 large tomatoes chopped**
**1 onion, chopped**
**1 bunch of cilantro**
**2 serrano or jalapeño chiles**
   **Juice of one lime**
**¼ cup orange juice**
**1 tablespoon rice wine vinegar**
**2 tablespoons olive oil**
**3 avocados chopped**

Blend the above ingredients together for a truly unique salsa.

# PEBBLE BEACH:
# POSH PLAYGROUND

DOÑA MARIA del Carmen Barreto was a bit of a romantic. She owned about 4,000 acres of an old Mexican land grant, El Pescadero.

It was a lovely piece of land, facing the Pacific Ocean on one side and bordered by Pacific Grove, Monterey and Carmel. But Doña Maria felt isolated in her country home. She wanted to join the fiestas and "look out on life and romance" in Monterey. So, in 1840, she sold El Pescadero for $500.

Today, that tract of land comprises most of the 5,300 acres of Pebble Beach. In fact, the Lodge at Pebble Beach now stands on part of El Pescadero (Spanish for the Fishing Place).

The extraordinarily beautiful land changed hands several times. Monterey land baron David Jacks bought the land, then sold it in 1879 for $35,000 to the Big Four railroad barons: Charles Crocker, Leland Stanford, Mark Hopkins and Collis Huntington.

THESE FOUR, who gained fame for their part in building the transcontinental railroad, formed the Pacific Improvement Company. At Crocker's urging, the company in 1880 built the fabulous Del Monte Hotel in Monterey. That luxurious hotel, which introduced tourism to the Monterey Peninsula, was so avant-garde that it boasted a telephone in every room. That was astonishing in 1880.

THE DEL MONTE Hotel was the original starting point of the 17 Mile Drive that led horse-drawn carriages through Monterey and Pacific Grove to the remote, wild country of Pebble Beach. Today, the old hotel is part of the Naval Postgraduate School and 17 Mile Drive is confined to 12 miles in Del Monte Forest, the proper name of the area commonly known as Pebble Beach.

THE EARLY TOURISTS were captivated by the wonderful coastline of rugged cliffs and sparkling blue water, the haunting, twisted Monterey cypress trees, and the beauty of the woodland trails. Many stopped to picnic at a particular beach full of shiny pebbles.

Another popular stop was at the Lone Cypress, a rare species of tree indigenous to the Del Monte Forest and Point Lobos. The Lone Cypress, bravely clinging to a rocky headland, has become perhaps the most photographed tree in the world. Robert Louis Stevenson called the wind-twisted cypresses "ghosts fleeing before the wind".

Enter Samuel Finley Brown Morse, a recent graduate of Yale University and grand-nephew of Samuel Finley Breese Morse, inventor of the telegraph.

THE AMBITIOUS young man became manager of the Pacific Improvement Company's properties. By that time, Pacific's assets included two run-down hotels, a golf course badly in need of repair, large tracts of undeveloped land and a sand mine. Everything except the sand mine was losing money.

Morse was convinced that the holding would become profitable, but the Big Four wanted to liquidate. They gave Morse, not yet 30, the opportunity to meet their asking price.

With help from San Francisco financier Herbert Fleishhacker, Morse came up with the $1.3 million asking price and Del Monte Properties Co. was formed in 1919.

MORSE HAD TWO key visions for Del Monte Forest: he considered it important that the forest be kept intact and he envisioned a series of golf courses.

Morse threw out a plan to build a large number of homes on small lots. And at a time when there were only 400 golf courses in America, he brought in golf pro Jack Neville to design the Pebble Beach championship golf course in 1918. Then he built two 18-hole courses, the Monterey Peninsula Country Club and the exclusive Cypress Point Golf Club. Thus began a Pebble Beach golf mecca that now includes Spyglass Hill, Poppy Hills and the Links at Spanish Bay.

BECAUSE LARGE NUMBERS of small homes were ruled out, more opulent homes, mansions and small palaces began to pop up in those pre-Depression days.

Posh homes included marble pillars, towers above the cliffs, gold plumbing fixtures, priceless antiques and art, swimming pools and, of course, high walls with imposing gates to keep out the curious.

One of the most imposing of the early mansions was the Macomber house, constructed in 1917. The huge structure was built almost entirely of logs. The estate covered more than 75 acres, overlooking Carmel Bay.

The living room, which also served as a ballroom, contained 1,800 square feet, larger than many modern homes. The dining room was 30 feet long, 30 feet wide and 30 feet high. Largely unoccupied for most of its existence, the log mansion burned down in 1977.

ANOTHER PEBBLE BEACH home along 17 Mile Drive is a scaled-down version of a Middle Eastern palace, complete with marble columns and a sand-bottomed swimming pool built on a ledge halfway down the cliff. The pool boasts radiant-heated sand to protect chilly toes on those foggy days so common along the coast.

One still hears stories about another of the forest's early buildings. It is said that the Canary Cottage was once a gambling casino that catered only to invited guests in evening clothes. What makes the tales of an exclusive casino more plausible is the pre-Depression influx of Hollywood types. The exclusivity of a posh Pacific playground between Hollywood and San Francisco drew many from the film colony to dress up for polo matches and elegant parties in a discreet setting.

AND BECAUSE Pebble Beach is so conscious of privacy (the forest has its own security force and charges an admission fee at the entry gates), tidbits of lore seem all the more delicious. Accounts from the turn of the century even speak of smugglers using Stillwater Cove to bring in opium, sake and illegal aliens. It is believed that the opium and sake ended up in the Chinatown that flourished for a time at Pacific Grove and Monterey.

ON DECEMBER 20, 1941, an unarmed American tanker ship, the Agwiworld, was attacked by a Japanese submarine off Cypress Point. The tanker managed to outmaneuver the sub and escape, but the incident resulted in a flood of wide-eyed accounts from the ship's crew and from astonished golfers who witnessed the attack while playing the Cypress Point course.

No account of Pebble Beach would be complete without Bing Crosby, who hosted his National Pro-Am Golf Championship, the Crosby Clambake, in Pebble Beach. Now called the AT&T Pebble Beach National Pro-Am, the tournament draws thousands of spectators each year in January. The tournament draws a wide range of sports figures, show biz personalities, and amateur and professional golfers to the Pebble Beach, Cypress Point and Spyglass Hill courses. For many fans, this is their only chance to see the exclusive courses.

Other prestigious events in Pebble Beach include the Concours d'Elegance, a classic car show, the Pebble Beach Summer Horse Show and the Pebble Beach Dressage Championships, the Del Monte Kennel Club Dog Show and the National Rugby Championships.

PEBBLE BEACH DATEBOOK: Spaulding Pro-Am Golf, January; AT&T National Pro-Am, January; Polo Matches, April; Del Monte Kennel Club Dog Show, May; National Rugby Tournament, May; Spring Horse Show, May; Concours d'Elegance, August; NCGA Amateur Golf, August; Summer Horse Show, August; California Challenge Polo Match, September; Almaden Senior Tennis Tournament, September; California Women's Amateur Golf, December.

# CLUB XIX

The Lodge at Pebble Beach
17 Mile Drive
Pebble Beach, CA 93953
(408)625-8519

CLUB XIX IS classically French, offering award-winning gourmet cuisine.

During the day this irresistible sidewalk bistro serves lunch either indoors or on the outside terrace overlooking the 18th green of Pebble Beach Golf Links. As the evening shadows move across the fairway, the dining mood is elegant, intimate and romantic.

A consistent winner of the Travel Holiday award, Club XIX features the finest fresh fish and produce Monterey has to offer.

The relaxed elegance of The Lodge extends to its 155 spacious guest rooms and six one-bedroom suites. All have either a private patio or balcony offering views of flowering gardens, seaside fairways or spectacular sunsets over Carmel Bay.

The Lodge at Pebble Beach. Since 1919, one of the outstanding resorts of the world.

*Chef Ron Patterson's Menu for Four*

*Brie en Croute*
*Cream of Spinach and Oyster Soup*
*Asparagus with Champagne Herb Vinaigrette*
*Lamb en Croute with Spinach Mousse in a Cognac Lamb Glace*
*Warm Apple Tarts*

# Brie en Croute

*Preparation Time: 25 Minutes*
*Pre-heat oven to 350°*

**Four 2½ oz. brie triangles**
**4 sheets puff pastry dough 4"x4"**
**1 teaspoon fresh rosemary, chopped**
**1 teaspoon fresh thyme, chopped**
**1 teaspoon fresh parsley, chopped**
**1 egg, whipped for wash**
**1 cup fresh raspberries**
**4 strawberries, fanned**
**4 sprigs rosemary**
**4 sprigs thyme**

Rub the chopped herbs over the brie pieces. Set each one on a square of puff dough, and place on a well-floured cutting board. Egg wash around the edges. Fold over all edges to meet on top. Cut away any excess and pat flat.

Flip the brie over; the bottom is now the top. Press a cross-hatched pattern into the dough with the back of a paring knife if desired. You can also decorate with shapes cut out of the excess dough.

Bake for 10-12 minutes at 350°.

Place on a plate and garnish with fresh herbs and fruit.

# Cream of Spinach and Oyster Soup

*Preparation Time: 30 Minutes*

1 cup fresh shucked oysters (4 reserved on the side)
1 small yellow onion, chopped
½ cup celery heart, chopped
2 bunches fresh spinach, cleaned and chopped
⅛ cup garlic, chopped
2 bay leaves
1 cup white wine
2 cups fish stock or clam sauce
1 cup heavy cream
½ teaspoon white pepper
1 oz. olive oil
1 pint whipped cream

Bring the olive oil up to sauté heat in a 4 quart soup pot. Add the onions, celery, garlic, bay leaves and white pepper. Add the oysters when the vegetables become translucent. Add the fish stock when oysters plump; also add white wine and cream. Reduce heat to simmer. Reduce mixture by ⅓. Add spinach and cook for a few minutes.

Remove from the stove and puree very fine with a food processor or blender. This can be done ahead and reheated before serving.

Fill each cup ¾ full and place one sautéed oyster in each cup (from the oysters held on the side). Place a dollop of plain whipped cream on top and brown in the broiler.

# Asparagus with Champagne Herb Vinaigrette

*Preparation Time: 30 Minutes (note refrigeration time)*

32 medium size asparagus spears
¾ cup Brut Champagne
¼ cup rice wine vinegar
  Juice of 4 lemons
¼ cup red onion, diced
 1 teaspoon fresh thyme, chopped
 1 teaspoon fresh dill, chopped
 1 teaspoon fresh parsley, chopped
¼ cup chives
 1 teaspoon coarse black pepper
 1 teaspoon superfine sugar
½ teaspoon salt
 2 eggs
 2 cups salad oil
¼ cup chopped egg white
¼ cup chopped egg yolk
¼ cup diced pimentos
¼ cup capers

In a blender add the Champagne, vinegar, lemon juice, red onion, thyme, dill, parsley, chives, pepper, sugar, salt, and two eggs. While blending, add the oil. Let the mixture set overnight for best flavor results.

Blanch the asparagus spears in boiling water. When the asparagus are tender, remove and submerse them in cold water. Cut each stalk the same length.

Place the asparagus spears in a row on a salad plate. Ladle approximately 1½ ounces of dressing across the middle of the spears.

Garnish with a small pile of egg yolk, egg white, diced pimentos and capers at the bottom of each spear.

# Lamb En Croute with Spinach Mousse in a Cognac Lamb Glace

*Preparation Time: 45 Minutes (note lamb stock cooking time)*
*Pre-heat oven to 350°*

**Four 4 oz. lamb loin halves**
**4 puff pastry sheets, 4"x6"**
**1 cup chopped frozen spinach**
**1 small onion, diced**
**1 tablespoon garlic, minced**
**1 teaspoon olive oil**
**1 egg**
**½ cup sour dough bread crumbs**
**¼ cup Marsala wine**
**Salt and pepper to taste**

Sauté the onions and garlic in olive oil. As onions become tender, add the spinach. Deglace with Marsala wine. Once the excess liquid has evaporated, remove from the heat and place in a food processor. Add egg, bread crumbs, salt and pepper. Puree at high speed. Let stand for 30 minutes.

Rub the lamb loin halves with coarse black pepper, salt and olive oil. Broil to rare.

With a small rubber spatula, spread ¼ inch of spinach mousse over the entire surface of each lamb loin. Envelope each with a puff pastry sheet. Seal each one with egg wash and coat the outside.

Bake the lamb en croutes at 350° 10-15 minutes, until golden brown.

Serve the lamb with sauce drizzled over the top. Wild rice is a excellent accompaniment to this dish.

# Cognac Lamb Glace

1 cup lamb demi glace
¼ cup minced shallots
½ cup cognac
¼ lb. sweet butter, room temperature
   Black pepper to taste

Prepare the lamb demi glace by combining lamb bones, carrots, onions, celery, garlic and thyme to make the lamb stock. No substitutes! (If this sauce is too much trouble, Dijon may be used).

Into a saucepan, put a pat of butter and saute shallots until they are soft.

Deglace with cognac away from the flame. After the liquid burns off, return to the heat. Reduce on low heat to a syrup consistency. Remove from the heat and pepper to taste. Whisk in the soft butter.

# Warm Apple Tarts

*Preparation Time: 30 Minutes*
*Pre-heat oven to 350°*

 2 Granny Smith apples
½ cup lemon juice
 2 cups pastry flour
½ cup powdered sugar
 2 whole eggs
 1 egg yolk
¼ lb. plus 4 teaspoons sweet butter
 1 teaspoon cinnamon
¼ cup superfine sugar
½ cup walnuts

Peel and core the apples. Slice them thin lengthwise and soak them in lemon juice.

Mix the flour and powdered sugar in a large bowl. Make a well, and add egg, yolk and butter. Knead to a dough consistency. Roll out with flour to ⅛ inch thick. Cut out circles and line into buttered individual tart molds. Fill the molds with the apple slices. Dab with pats of butter and sprinkle with cinnamon, superfine sugar and walnuts.

Bake at 350° for 10-12 minutes.

# Topping

½ cup heavy cream
 1 oz. brandy
  Dash of nutmeg
4 mint leaves

Whip the cream, brandy and nutmeg until firm. Place a dollop of the topping on the tart and garnish with a mint leaf.

# THE BAY CLUB RESTAURANT

The Inn at Spanish Bay
2700 17-Mile Drive
Pebble Beach, CA 93953
(408)647-7500

THE BAY CLUB, Pebble Beach's newest restaurant, features delightful Mediterranean cuisine with five star elegance.

Contributing to its gracious ambience are shaded earth tones with accents of olive green, intimate banquettes and an impressive display of fine wines.

Accommodations offer 270 luxurious rooms and suites in an elegant and almost indulgent sense of retreat.

Each room has its own fireplace, custom made furnishings and four-poster beds topped with quilted down comforters. Most guest rooms offer a private balcony or patio, and in every case views are magnificent.

Gracious hospitality, exemplary service and unequaled dining amid scenic grandeur of extravagant proportions.

*Chef Christian Schmidt's Menu for Four*

Grilled Prawns with Pancetta
Salad De Bay Club
Veal Medallions with Diced Prosciutto and Artichokes Marsala

# Grilled Prawns with Pancetta

*Preparation Time: 20 Minutes*

16 gulf prawns
16 slices pancetta bacon
 1 head oriental purple kale, julienne
 1 tablespoon shallots, sliced thin
 6 tablespoons butter
½ cup vermouth
 2 tablespoons lemon juice
   Salt and pepper to taste
 4 sprigs of Italian parsley

Peel and devein the shrimps, leaving the tails on. Wrap the bacon around the prawns and grill until cooked. Set aside.

Sauté the kale and shallots in 1 tablespoon butter. Add the vermouth and lemon juice. Remove the pan from the heat and whip the rest of the butter into the mixture until it becomes a smooth creamy butter sauce. Salt and pepper to taste.

Place the sauce mixture on a plate and top with the prawns. Garnish with parsley.

# Salad De Bay Club

*Preparation Time: 25 Minutes*

  4 sheets of puff pastry shells
  8 handfuls mixed greens
20 nasturtium (edible flowers)
½ cup Gewurztraminer
  1 cup heavy cream
  4 tablespoons shallots
  2 tablespoons thyme
  2 tablespoons rice vinegar
½ cup plus 2 tablespoons gruyere cheese, grated
    Salt and pepper to taste

Heat the pastry shells according to directions.

Combine the Gewurztraminer, cream, shallots, thyme and rice vinegar. Bring the mixture to a boil and reduce slowly to half the amount. Add ½ cup of the cheese and whip it into the dressing. Salt and pepper to taste.

Place the lettuce on a dinner plate and top with the hot pastry shells. Pour the dressing in the shells and sprinkle the rest of the gruyere cheese on top of the dressing.

Garnish with the edible flowers around the lettuce.

# Veal Medallions
# with Diced Prosciutto
# and Artichokes Marsala

*Preparation Time: 25 Minutes*

**Four 12 oz. veal medallions**
**½ cup prosciutto, diced**
**4 tablespoons shallots**
**¾ cup artichoke bottoms, diced**
**1 oz. butter**
**½ cup Marsala wine**
**1 cup veal stock**
**½ cup tomatoes, peeled, seeded and diced**
**3 tablespoons chives**
**Salt and pepper to taste**
**1 bunch watercress**

Sauté the veal medallions quickly in a hot pan. Set the veal aside.

Sauté the shallots, prosciutto and artichoke bottoms in butter. Add the Marsala wine and veal stock and reduce for 2 minutes. Add the tomatoes and chives. Salt and pepper to taste

Present on a dinner plate with watercress garnish.

# CARMEL:
# CHIC TO CHIC

YES, VIRGINIA, there was a Carmel before Clint Eastwood came along.

When the actor-director-restaurateur became mayor of the one-square mile village in 1986, his fame drew so many fans that the city council had to move its meetings out of city hall and into a larger facility.

And even today, with Eastwood no longer in office, the most frequent question asked by visitors is a sheepish, "Where's Clint's place?"

Most of the tourists were hoping to catch a glimpse of Eastwood at the Hog's Breath Inn, of which he is a part owner. But Eastwood, who likes his privacy, rarely visited the Hog's Breath. Instead, he bought the Mission Ranch, just outside the city limits, so he could have a place to enjoy dinner in private.

THE LOCATION for Carmel-by-the-Sea was determined in 1771, when Father Junipero Serra moved his mission from Monterey to Carmel. Serra preferred the new location because it offered more fertile land and fresh water.

Using converted Indians as laborers, Serra built the mission and called it Mission San Carlos Borromeo del Rio Carmelo. Still boasting an off-center front window, it is better known as the Carmel Mission Basilica. After his death, Serra was buried at the mission and, in recent years, a growing movement is advocating the declaration of Serra as a saint of the Roman Catholic Church. Pope John Paul II visited the mission in 1987 and blessed Serra's grave.

THE CITY GOT its start in the late 1880s when Santiago Duckworth, a real estate agent, dreamed of establishing a Catholic resort community to rival the popular Methodist Retreat at Pacific Grove. Working out an agreement with land owner Honore Escolle, Duckworth started selling lots. The first two homes belonged to Davenport Bromfield and Delos Goldsmith (these names are real, honest).

By the turn of the century, the concept of another religious retreat was forgotten. Then along came San Francisco attorney Frank Powers and real estate agent J. Frank Devendorf, who formed the Carmel Development Co., with holdings approximating the present area of the village. These two developers encouraged people of modest means who were interested in the arts. Many a lot was sold for nothing down, pay when you can.

By 1903, the village consisted of 100 people. A population surge occurred in 1885, when David Starr Jordan, president of Stanford University, encouraged professors from Stanford and the University of California to move to Carmel. So many of them moved there that a section near the waterfront came to be called Faculty Row.

ANOTHER SURGE occurred after 1906, when the San Francisco earthquake and fire left homeless a group of artists, musicians and writers. Poet George Sterling and fiery novelist Mary Austin attracted the homeless artists to Carmel. With the Victorian era just ended, the bohemian antics of the free-spirited artists is said to have shocked Carmel residents. Particularly scandalous were the reports of moonlight abalone and mussel feeds, where many jugs of red wine were consumed and barefoot women let loose their long hair as they danced around bonfires in the woods.

THE LONG TRADITION of Carmel as a haven for artists and characters had been born. Their presence set the pattern for the town as a cultural community of free spirits dedicated to preserving their surroundings and the village's unique charm.

The desire to protect the wooded charms of Carmel-by-the-Sea was established with incorporation in 1916. A law dating from that time bans the cutting of trees. Not even a branch of a city-owned tree can be cut unless approved by a commission and permission must be obtained to remove any tree on private property.

A key moment in the preservation of Carmel came with passage of a far-reaching zoning ordinance in 1929. The ordinance dictated that the residential nature of the village should always be more important than business development.

THE ORDINANCE HELPED keep Carmel Beach free of commercial development. The height of buildings was limited, neon and electric signs were prohibited and street lights and sidewalks were discouraged in residential areas.

You may notice that many of the homes in Carmel sport signs with quaint names. That's because Carmel homes have no house numbers. Neither is there any home delivery of mail; residents pick up their mail at the post office and use the occasion to socialize and keep up on the latest gossip.

Another feature that sets Carmel aside are its fairy-tale cottages. Their story began in the 1920s with Mayotta Comstock. Mrs. Comstock made dolls of rags and felt. Her creations were so popular that they drew buyers from all over. The Comstock home was crammed with dolls, so Mayotta convinced her husband, Hugh, to build a large "doll house" in the woods so she could display her dolls. The person-sized house became all the rage and soon merchants wanted doll houses of their own. Perhaps the best known of these is the Tuck Box Tea Room on Ocean Ave.

CARMEL HAS MORE shops than you can shake a credit card at. Scores of shops include upscale boutiques, jewelry shops, antique stores, specialty stores that range from designer toys to handicrafts, art and photography galleries, a large number of chic restaurants and the ever-present Clint Eastwood paraphernalia parlors.

ONE IMPORTANT THING to remember about spending the day in Carmel is that parking space is at a premium. Many parking meters are for short time limits and parking tickets are a large source of income for the village. Car-pooling and parking in garages are recommended.

Special events abound in Carmel. Foremost among the musical events is the prestigious Carmel Bach Festival, founded in 1935. The weeklong programs, staged in July and August, are dedicated to the works of Johann Sebastian Bach, his contemporaries and works of composers influenced by Bach.

Performances are still staged at the Forest Theater, which was founded in 1910 and became city property in 1937. The original stage productions involved most of the townspeople. The Forest Theater was California's first outdoor community theater.

ANOTHER NOTEWORTHY event is the Great Sand Castle Contest, usually held on a Sunday in October at Carmel Beach. Sponsored by a group of architects, the beach blossoms every year with fanciful sand creations and castles, most based on the theme of the year. In order to avoid large crowds, the date of the event and its theme are closely-guarded secrets that are released to the press just a week before the fun-filled event. Bribing of the judges is not only condoned, but actively encouraged.

One last tip: traffic on Highway 1 gets jammed up every afternoon during rush hour, especially in the summer months. Wise visitors plan to stay off Highway 1 just outside Carmel during the commute hours and avoid the Ocean Ave. exit, preferring the Carpenter Street exit.

CARMEL DATEBOOK: Carmel Bach Festival, July and August; Fiesta de San Carlos Borromeo at Carmel Mission Basilica, September; Great Sand Castle Contest, October; Halloween Parade and Carmel Birthday Party, October.

# THE COBBLESTONE INN

Junipero between 7th & 8th
P.O. Box 3185
Carmel, CA 93921
(408)625-5222
800-222-4667

THIS SPECIAL INN has a fresh country atmosphere, with a fireplace, telephone, private bath and color television in each of the 24 rooms. Fresh flowers and other amenities will make you feel at home, as will the comfortable sitting area. Quilts, assorted pillows, handsome antiques and fresh fruit are but a few of the guest comforts.

In the morning, a generous breakfast is tastefully prepared and served in the dining room or on the terrace of the courtyard.

You are also invited to cross the courtyard to the main living room and lounge where guests gather in front of the large stone fireplace to enjoy complimentary tea, sherry, wine and delicious hors d'oeuvres.

# Mexican Eggs

*Preparation Time: 10 Minutes*
*Serves 4*

   6 eggs
   2 tablespoons melted butter
   ¼ cup flour
   1 teaspoon baking soda
   1 small can green chiles
   2 cups cottage cheese
   2 cups grated cheddar cheese

   Whisk together first 4 ingredients and cook over medium heat. Add
the chiles and cheeses before stirring.

# Double Corn and Cheese Muffins

*Preparation Time: 30 Minutes*
*Pre-heat oven to 400°*
*Yield: 18 Muffins*

1⅓ cups flour
   1 tablespoon baking powder
   1 teaspoon salt
   2 tablespoons sugar
   ¾ cup cornmeal
   2 eggs
   1 cup milk
   ¼ cup oil
   1 cup creamed corn niblets
   ¼ teaspoon rosemary
   ½ green onion, chopped
   2 cups grated cheddar
   ½ cup diced green chiles.

   Combine the dry ingredients with the liquid ingredients and add
the onions, chiles and cheese. Stir lightly until blended. Bake in greased
muffin cups at 400° for 20 minutes.

# Basil Chicken Pâté

*Preparation Time: One hour*
*Pre-heat oven to 350°*
*Yields: 5 mini loaves or one standard loaf*

2 medium yellow onions, chopped
1 clove garlic, chopped
2 tablespoons butter
4 lbs. raw chicken breasts
   Half of a red pepper
3 egg whites
2½ cups cream
1 bunch parsley
½ cup packed fresh basil
   Salt and pepper

Sauté the onions and garlic in butter. In a food processor puree the chicken in 2 batches adding half the cream. Add the onion mixture and egg whites. Process the other half of the chicken, adding the rest of the cream and salt and pepper. Process until chopped. Add ⅓ of the chicken mixture to the parsley and basil. Season with salt and pepper. Process.

Start with the white chicken mixture and spread on the bottom of the bread pan. Next place a few strips of the red pepper on the top. Add the green mixture then the red pepper strips, ending with the white mixture on the top.

Place the pâté pan in another pan filled with water. Cover both pans with foil and bake at 350° for 35-45 minutes.

# Spinach and Feta Cheese Triangles

*Preparation Time: 45 Minutes (note refrigeration time)*
*Pre-heat oven to 400°*
*Yields: 35-40*

4 tablespoons oil
3 onions, finely chopped
24 oz. spinach, thawed and drained
2 tablespoons dill
8 oz. feta cheese, crumbled
2 eggs, beaten
6 tablespoons sour cream
Salt and pepper
Dash of nutmeg
Puff pastry

Sauté the onions in oil until tender. Stir in the spinach. Cook 5 minutes longer. Stir in the dill and cheese. Cool. Mix in the eggs, sour cream, nutmeg and season with salt and pepper. Refrigerate until cold.

Cut the puff pastry into 4" squares. Place on a sheet pan with one tablespoon of filling in the center of the pastry. Fold the opposite corners over to form a triangle. Press the edges together with a fork to seal.

Bake at 400° for 15-20 minutes.

# SAN ANTONIO HOUSE

San Antonio between Ocean & 7th
P.O. Box 2747
Carmel, CA 93921
(408)624-4334


NESTLED BEHIND AN ivy-covered wall, turn of the century Carmel heritage abounds. Sophisticated and yet casual, amidst the excitement of the Carmel Beach and bustling village, San Antonio House offers romantic seclusion.

Two- and three-room suites are complemented by antiques and a private collection of artwork. Each suite has a private entrance, bath, fireplace and stone patio.

San Antonio House is surrounded by flowering shrubs, expansive tree-shaded lawns, flower-lined walkways and Carmel stone patios and terraces. The gardens are a captivating place to take in the sun and the sound of the sea.

San Antonio House
Carmel-By-The-Sea, Calif.

# Buttermilk Bran Muffins

*Preparation Time: 15 Minutes*
*Yields: 2½ dozen muffins*

**Half of a 15 oz. box raisin bran cereal**
**2½ cups flour**
  **2 cups sugar**
  **1 teaspoon salt**
  **2 teaspoons baking soda**
  **1 teaspoon baking powder**
  **1 teaspoon cinnamon**
  **1 apple, chopped**
  **2 eggs, beaten**
  **½ quart buttermilk**
  **1 cube margarine**
  **½ cup raisins**

Mix all the dry ingredients and add the beaten eggs, buttermilk and margarine. Mix well. Add the raisins and apples.

Pour the mixture into greased muffin tins. Bake 25 minutes at 350°.

Remove from the oven and cool. Drizzle the mixed topping over the muffins.

# Topping

**½ cup flour**
**½ cup sugar**
**½ cube margarine**
  **1 teaspoon cinnamon**
**½ teaspoon nutmeg**
**¼ teaspoon ginger**

Combine the above ingredients for the muffin topping.

# THE SANDPIPER INN

2408 Bay View Ave.
Carmel, CA 93923
(408)624-6433
800-633-6433

WELCOMING GUESTS WITH warm and gracious hospitality since 1929, the Sandpiper Inn is a romantic bed and breakfast inn, just fifty yards from Carmel Beach.

The inn has 15 individually decorated rooms, furnished with handsome country antiques, fresh flowers and private baths. Many rooms have outstanding ocean views with wood-burning fireplaces.

The comfortable lounge—with cathedral ceilings and Carmel stone fireplace—is the heart of the Inn, where guests enjoy a complimentary continental breakfast and afternoon sherry.

A small, well-stocked library and ten-speed bicycles are available for your enjoyment.

# Cranberry Orange Muffins

*Preparation Time: 30 Minutes*
*Pre-heat oven to 375°*
*Yield: 18 Muffins*

2 cups fresh cranberries, chopped
⅓ cup sugar
6 tablespoons orange juice
1 tablespoon orange rind, grated
½ cup margarine
1 cup sugar
1 egg
2 cups flour
1 teaspoon baking powder
½ teaspoon baking soda
½ teaspoon salt

Mix the cranberries with ⅓ cup sugar, orange juice and rind. Set aside.

Cream the margarine adding 1 cup sugar and beaten egg. Add sifted dry ingredients to creamed mixture. Gently mix in cranberries.

Fill greased muffin cups ¾ full. Bake at 375° for 20 minutes.

# SEA VIEW INN

Camino Real between 11th and 12th
P.O. Box 4138
Carmel, CA 93921
(408)624-8778

WELCOMING GUESTS FOR over 60 years, the Sea View Inn has been completely restored, retaining the nostalgic homelike atmosphere of a traditional country inn.

Featured in Harper's Bazaar as a "place to take your lover", the Sea View Inn is a quiet, cozy Victorian with 8 individually decorated rooms furnished with antiques, 6 with private baths.

A generous continental breakfast is served by the fireside, as well as afternoon tea and coffee, and wine in the evening.

The Sea View Inn is located 3 blocks from the beach and 6 blocks from the village.

*Sea View Inn*

# Quiche a la Sea View

*Preparation Time: 30 Minutes*
*Pre-heat oven to 350°*

9" pie shell
 1 cup chopped Swiss cheese
 ¼ cup grated parmesan cheese
 1 tablespoon dried chives
 2 eggs, beaten
 1 cup half & half
 ¼ teaspoon salt
 ⅛ teaspoon pepper
 ⅛ teaspoon nutmeg

Pre-bake pie shell for 5 minutes.
Fill the shell with mixture of Swiss cheese, parmesan cheese and chives. Set aside.
Blend the eggs, cream and seasoning. Pour into a pie shell and bake at 450° for 10 minutes. Reduce the heat to 350° and bake 10 minutes longer, or until set.

# STONEHOUSE INN

8th below Monte Verde
P.O. Box 2517
Carmel, CA 93921
(408)624-4569

THIS SPECIAL HOUSE has a stone exterior, hand shaped by local Indians when it was built in 1906. A glass-enclosed front porch with comfortable seating is seen as you enter the front door.

The restful bedrooms, with shared baths, are light and airy, and some have a view of the ocean through the trees. Each room is decorated in soft colors featuring antiques, cozy quilts, fresh fruit and special touches for guest comfort.

A generous breakfast is served each morning in the sunny dining room, in the peaceful garden or before the fire.

# Strawberry Banana Bread

*Preparation Time: 1½ Hours*
*Pre-heat oven to 350°*
*Yield: One Loaf*

1½ cups sifted flour
⅔ cup sugar
2 teaspoons baking powder
½ teaspoon salt
¾ cup quick-cooking oats
⅓ cup oil
2 eggs, lightly beaten
½ cup strawberries, mashed
½ cup bananas, mashed
¼ cup almonds, diced

In a medium mixing bowl, sift together the flour, sugar, baking powder and salt; stir in the oats. Add the oil, eggs, strawberries, banana and almonds, stirring just until no dry ingredients show.

Turn into a greased 8½"x4½"x2½" loaf pan. Bake at 350° for one hour or until a wooden pick inserted in the center comes out clean.

Cool on a wire rack 10 minutes, then turn out of the pan to complete cooling.

# VAGABOND'S HOUSE INN

4th and Dolores
P.O. Box 2747
Carmel, CA 93921
(408)624-7738

SITUATED IN THE heart of the village of Carmel, this charming brick half-timbered English Tudor country inn is a delightful experience. It begins as you walk up the front steps to enter an atmosphere that seems almost magical. You'll find yourself in a courtyard dominated by old and very large oak trees, lush with camellias, rhododendrons, hanging plants, ferns and flowers in great profusion.

Accommodations include 11 unique suites, each with a fireplace and private bath. A continental breakfast will be served in your room or in the courtyard each morning.

Vagabond's House is located in the midst of Carmel's finest restaurants, unique shops and well-known art galleries.

Vagabond's House
Carmel-By-The-Sea, California

# Cheesy Potatoes

*Preparation Time: 1½ Hours*
*Serves 4*

2 lbs. potatoes, cooked and shredded
6 oz. shredded sharp cheese
6 green onions, sliced
6 eggs
2 cups milk
1 cup sour cream
   Salt and pepper to taste

   Layer the potatoes, cheese and onions in a 9"x13" baking dish.
   Mix in a pouring bowl, the eggs, milk, sour cream, salt and pepper.
   Pour the mixture over the potatoes, and bake uncovered at 350° for
one hour.

# CREME CARMEL

San Carlos and 7th Street
P.O. Box 2916
Carmel, CA 93921
(408)624-0444

EXCELLENT SEASONAL CUISINE sums up the philosophy of owner-chef, Craig Ling. He uses only the finest ingredients available to inspire many creative and tasteful dishes.

Dining at Creme Carmel will delight the most discriminating palate as well as the most ardent romantic. The setting is Country French; simple, charming yet elegant. White table linens and china are the backdrop for the extraordinary cuisine.

The service is first class and unpretentious. The wine list is well chosen. Reservations are recommended.

## *Chef Craig Ling's Menu for Six*

*Maine Lobster Soup with Water Chestnuts and Baby Corn*
*Lamb Loin with Rosemary and Garlic*
*Apple Mint Chutney*
*Chocolate Soufflé*

# Maine Lobster Soup with Water Chestnuts and Baby Corn

*Preparation Time: 1½ Hours*

Two 1 lb. lobsters
1 onion
2 carrots
3 celery ribs
1 bay leaf
12 peppercorns
¼ lemon
1 teaspoon thyme
6 cloves
1 tablespoon paprika
1 cup sherry

Pinch cayenne pepper
6 fresh water chestnuts, peeled and chopped
6 ears baby corn, or 2 ears fresh sweet corn shaved from cob
Meat from lobsters, chopped
Salt and white pepper to taste

Chop the vegetables and cover with enough water to also cover lobsters. Bring the water to a boil. Put the lobsters in boiling water for 3 minutes. Remove the pot from the stove and let stand for 15 minutes. Remove lobsters. When cool, remove meat from the tail and claws and refrigerate. Put the shells back into the water and boil for 45 minutes. Strain out and reserve all the liquid. Add sherry and seasonings, then reduce liquid to about 2 quarts.

Five minutes before serving, add the chestnuts and corn. Two minutes before serving, add the chopped lobster.

For a richer, creamy lobster soup, thicken with roux and add some cream or half and half.

# Lamb Loin with Rosemary and Garlic

*Preparation Time: 20 Minutes (note cooking time)*
*Pre-heat oven to 400°*

3 boned lamb loins
(approximately 2 lbs.)
2 tablespoons rosemary,
finely chopped
4 cloves garlic, pressed
3 cups lamb/veal stock

1 cup white wine
½ tomato, peeled, seeded
and diced
2 tablespoons butter
2 tablespoons flour

Make the sauce first by making roux with butter and flour. Cook over low heat until nutty brown. Add the wine, stock, rosemary, garlic and tomatoes. Boil gently until reduced by ⅓.

Lightly oil a large skillet and sear lamb for 10 seconds on all sides. Place the lamb on a rack with a pan under the rack, in the oven. Place the rosemary and garlic on each loin. Bake at 400° to desired doneness (8 minutes for medium rare).

Slice and add sauce.

# Apple-Mint Chutney

*Preparation Time: 25 Minutes*

4 Granny Smith apples,
chopped
½ cup onion, finely chopped
2 garlic cloves, pressed
3 tablespoons fresh mint,
chopped

1½ teaspoons dried tarragon
⅛ teaspoon white pepper
A pinch of nutmeg
1 cup white wine vinegar
⅓ cup white wine
⅓ cup sugar

Combine all the ingredients except the sugar and cook in a large skillet over medium high heat until most of the liquid is gone. Add the sugar. Cook and stir 3 more minutes.

Cool and refrigerate.

# Chocolate Soufflé

*Preparation Time: 35 Minutes*
*Pre-heat oven to 375°*

 **6 tablespoons butter**
**½ cup flour**
**½ cup milk**
**⅓ cup cream**
**⅔ cup sugar**
   **Whiskey and cognac to equal ⅓ cup**
 **6 eggs, separated**
 **7 oz. bittersweet chocolate**

Cook the butter and flour gently for 5 minutes. Add the milk and cream all at once. Cook over medium heat, stirring frequently for 10 minutes.

While cooking the milk, melt the chocolate in a mixing bowl over hot water. When the milk is very thick and sticky add whiskey, cognac and sugar. Cook 3 more minutes.

Separate the eggs, putting the yolks into a mixing bowl. While stirring the chocolate, add the milk mixture. When completely mixed, stir yolks and add the chocolate mixture.

Whip the egg whites with a pinch of salt until stiff. Fold into the chocolate mixture.

Bake at 375° for 15 minutes in individual dishes.

# THE FRENCH POODLE RESTAURANT

Junipero and 5th Ave.
Carmel, CA 93921
(408)624-8643

AUTHENTIC AND SAVORY French cuisine served graciously, is a delightful experience in this highly-rated restaurant.

In addition to the traditional French menu, spa cuisine is emphasized along with a multitude of options for light dinners.

Pastel colors, candlelight, linen and fresh flowers create a distinctive ambience in a comfortable and inviting dining room.

 The French Poodle

*Owner-Chef Marc Vedrines' Menu for Four*

*Breast of Duck Veiled in Old Port*
*Spring Chicken in Chablis*
*Creme Renuersee a L'Orange*

# Breast of Duck Veiled in Old Port

*Preparation Time: One Hour*

    2 ducks (culver ducks)
    2 cups game stock
¼ lb. butter
    2 cups red port
    1 cup wild rice
1¼ tablespoons onion, finely chopped
    Salt and pepper to taste
    1 cup water.

Lift off the breast of duck and trim the excess fat. Sauté the duck breasts in 2 tablespoons butter until golden. Sprinkle with salt and pepper, cooking 5 minutes on each side. They should still be pink in the middle.

Heat the port in saucepan adding the game stock until the liquid becomes syrupy. Add six tablespoons of butter. Pass sauce through a sieve.

Sauté the wild rice and onions in 3 tablespoons butter, adding 2 cups of water or stock. Cover and cook for 45 minutes.

Slice and arrange duck breasts on wild rice. Pour sauce over breasts and serve.

# Spring Chicken in Chablis

*Preparation Time: 1½ Hours*

**2½ lb. fryer chicken**
   **Flour as needed**
 **6 oz. butter or margarine**
**12 mushroom caps**
 **2 tablespoons shallots, minced**
 **1 teaspoon garlic cloves, crushed**
 **½ teaspoon thyme**
**12 oz. Chablis**
 **2 cups chicken broth**
   **Salt and pepper to taste**
   **Truffles and chopped parsley for garnish**

Disjoint the chicken and sprinkle with seasonings as desired. Dust lightly with flour and sauté in butter or margarine until golden. Add the mushroom caps, shallots, thyme and garlic and simmer for 3 minutes. Add the Chablis and simmer covered for 5 minutes. Add the chicken broth and cook for 30 minutes.

Remove the chicken and mushrooms and heat the sauce until reduced by one-fifth.

Strain over the chicken and garnish with truffles and chopped parsley.

# Creme Renuersée à L'Orange

*Preparation Time: One Hour*
*Pre-heat oven to 400°*
*Serves 12*

 4 cups sugar
½ cup water
 1 quart milk
 1 teaspoon pure vanilla extract
 6 egg yolks
 6 whole eggs
 2 oz. orange rind, grated
 3 oz. orange-flavored liqueur

Combine 2 cups of sugar with water and pour into 12 ramekins. Set aside.

Mix egg yolks, eggs and 1 cup sugar in a bowl. Set aside.

Heat milk, 1 cup of sugar and vanilla to boiling. Add the orange rind and orange-flavored liqueur to boiling milk mixture. Slowly combine with the egg yolk mixture and beat together. Pass through a sieve and pour in the ramekins.

Bake at 400° for 40 minutes. Refrigerate.

Before serving, let stand for 20 minutes.

# Jimmy's American Place

26344 Carmel Rancho Lane
Carmel, CA 93923
(408)625-6666

THE ULTIMATE 50'S Diner. Flashy neon and chrome, glazed black and white tile and fantastic food that's fun to eat. You have arrived at Jimmy's American Place!

Select from a variety of oysters at the oyster bar. Or munch on garlic, basil and pine nut pizelle. How about herbed smoked spicy prawns in melon relish, or blackened catfish with cornmeal cakes? Try roast garlic chicken with mashed potatoes and gravy or sip on Jimmy's hot martini. Need we say more?

This popular restaurant is open for lunch and dinner.

OYSTER BAR • AMERICAN REGIONAL CUISINE
OAK GRILLED SEAFOOD & MEATS • SPIRITS

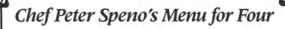

## Chef Peter Speno's Menu for Four

*Pizelle*
*Fried Oysters with Jalapeño Cream Sauce*
*Steamed Mussels in Tarragon*

# Pizelle

*Preparation Time: 15 Minutes*
*Pre-heat oven to 500°*

**10" flour tortilla**
 **8 oz. tomato sauce**
**¼ cup fresh basil, finely minced**
**¼ cup fresh oregano, finely minced**
 **2 cloves garlic, minced**
 **4 oz. mozzarella, thinly sliced**
 **5 strips sun-dried tomatoes**
 **5 fresh basil leaves**
 **2 tablespoons pine nuts**

Combine basil, oregano and garlic into tomato sauce. Spread thinly onto tortilla and cover with a single layer of mozzarella. Decorate with pine nuts and sun-dried tomatoes.

Bake for 8 minutes or until the cheese is bubbly and tortilla is golden brown.

Remove from the oven and decorate with fresh basil. Cut into wedges with a pizza cutter.

# Fried Oysters with Jalapeño Cream Sauce

*Preparation Time: 15 Minutes*

**12 Maryland Bluepoint oysters, shucked (save bottom shell)**
**½ cup flour**
 **1 teaspoon salt**
 **1 teaspoon black pepper**
**½ cup vegetable oil**
**½ cup cream**
 **1 jalapeño sliced in half**
   **Lime**

Combine flour with salt and pepper. Dredge oysters in the flour mixture and place in heated skillet with oil. When edges turn brown, cook for 2 minutes longer. Do not overcook.

Pour cream in a heavy saucepan with jalapeño and reduce by half. Add salt and pepper to taste. Remove the jalapeño and squeeze in juice of ½ the lime.

Place oyster shells on large round plate filled with rock salt. Spoon in jalapeño sauce, then place oyster on each shell. Garnish with lime wedges.

# Steamed Mussels in Tarragon

*Preparation Time: 15 Minutes*

4 lbs. mussels, scrubbed and debearded
8 oz. clam juice
½ cup white wine
1 teaspoon garlic, minced
1 teaspoon shallots, minced
¼ cup tarragon, chopped
1 tablespoon butter
¼ cup cream

In a heavy saucepan, over medium heat, combine wine, clam juice, garlic, shallots and mussels. Cook until mussels open. Remove from the heat and add butter and cream.

Arrange mussels in a bowl and pour in sauce. Sprinkle with tarragon and serve.

# ON THE PARK BAR AND GRILL

Junipero at 6th Ave.
Carmel, CA 93921
(408)625-1766

AN ARRAY OF international and California delicacies in a comfortable, elegant and fun ambience best describes On The Park Bar and Grill, one of Carmel's newest and most talked about dining establishments.

Wooden floors, brass trimmings, plants and a big warm fireplace add to the comfortable, elegant environment.

Veal Paillarde stuffed with prosciutto and fontina cheese, or grilled lamb steak with mint pesto are examples of the creations of Chef Terry Teplitzky, who brings extensive training from the finest restaurants in Washington D.C. and San Francisco to On The Park.

For lighter appetites, the menu also offers Spa Cuisine, which features healthy selections of steamed vegetables with fresh fish or chicken.

> ## Chef Terry Teplitzky's Menu for Six
> *Maryland Crabcake with Wasabi Ginger Mayonnaise*
> *Rainbow Trout with Thai Vegetable Sauce*
> *Coconut Caramel Custard*

# Maryland Crabcake with Wasabi Ginger Mayonnaise

*Preparation Time: 30 Minutes*

1 lb. Blue crabmeat
½ red pepper, diced
½ green pepper, diced
2 green onions, sliced thin
1 tablespoon Dijon mustard
1 tablespoon breadcrumbs

6 dashes Tabasco
5 dashes Worcestershire sauce
1 oz. cream
Flour and butter for frying

Add all ingredients in a large bowl, making sure not to squeeze crab and break up lumps. Divide into 6 equal amounts and press to form cakes.

Pat with flour and sauté in clarified butter until brown. Turn over and brown the other side.

# Wasabi Ginger Mayonnaise

1 cup mayonnaise
1-inch piece ginger grated
1 tablespoon wasabi
Juice of lemon
2 tablespoons soy sauce

Mix all the ingredients together. Adjust seasonings to your own tastes.

147

# Rainbow Trout with Thai Vegetable Sauce

*Preparation Time: 45 Minutes*

  6 boneless rainbow trout
  ¼ cup soy sauce
  ¼ cup corn starch
  ½ cup oil

Dip the trout in soy to coat skin then dredge in the cornstarch. Deep fry in 375° oil for approximately 8 minutes.

# Thai Vegetable Sauce

  ¾ cup soy sauce
  ¾ cup rice vinegar
  ¾ cup sugar
  ⅓ cup ketchup
1¼ cup chicken stock
2-inch ginger, sliced
  1 onion, sliced
  1 cup carrots, julienne
  1 cup celery, julienne
  1 cup leeks, julienne
  1 cup red pepper julienne
  1 cup shiitake mushrooms, sliced

Combine all of the above ingredients, except the vegetables, and bring to a boil. Simmer for 15 minutes.

Add the vegetables and bring the sauce back to a boil. Simmer 5 minutes and serve over trout.

# Coconut Caramel Custard

*Preparation Time: 1½ Hours*
*Pre-heat oven to 350°*

1½ cups sugar
  2 tablespoons water
2¼ cups milk
  3 eggs, beaten
  4 egg yolks, beaten
  ⅓ cup sugar
1½ tablespoons almond extract
  ½ cup toasted unsweetened coconut
    Garnish with whipped cream

Combine sugar and water in saucepan over high heat and bring to a boil. Cook until sugar caramelizes. Pour into custard cup and cool.

Combine sugar, almond extract and coconut in bowl and set aside.

Bring milk to a boil and pour in the beaten eggs and blend. Combine both bowls and pour into six custard cups.

Place custard cup in a large pan, filled halfway with hot water and bake at 350° for 45 minutes, or until skewer placed in custard comes out clean.

Let cool. Unmold onto individual plates and garnish with whipped cream.

Custard can be made one week in advance.

# PACIFIC'S EDGE RESTAURANT

Highlands Inn
P.O. Box 1700
Carmel, CA 93921
(408)624-3801


PACIFIC'S EDGE RESTAURANT, located in the Highlands Inn at the edge of Big Sur and minutes from Carmel, offers spectacular ocean and coastal views. You will dine in an open and inviting room where you can watch the rolling Pacific swells surge toward shore. Every evening provides a dramatic sunset, giving way to a million stars.

The Executive Chef specializes in presenting the freshest and finest California cuisines, carefully prepared with Salinas Valley produce, California meats and poultry and Monterey Bay seafood.

Laced throughout the inn's wooded acres are flowering walkways, hidden hot tubs and scores of cottages and townhouses. Each accommodation includes a wood-burning fireplace and vista deck.

The townhouse units offer a custom-furnished parlor, full kitchen, master bedroom and bath with a massive spa tub.

Visit soon!

# HIGHLANDS INN

*Chef Don Ferch's Menu for Four*

Mussel Bisque
Spicy Grilled Seabass with Peach Salsa
Sautéed Mushrooms with Young Lettuce and Goat Cheese
Grilled Vegetables
Terrine of Chocolate

# Mussel Bisque

*Preparation Time: 45 Minutes*

**2 lbs. mussels**
**2 shallots**
**2 garlic cloves**
**2 celery stalks**
**2 carrots**
**1 pint white wine**
**2 sprigs thyme**
**2 pints clam juice**
**2 cups cream**
**2 tablespoons butter**
   **Salt and pepper to taste**

Wash mussels in cold water. In a large pot, sauté the shallots, garlic, carrots and celery in butter for 2 minutes. Add the cleaned mussels and half of the wine. Cover and steam 5 minutes.

Remove mussels and all shells. Add the remaining wine, herbs and clam juice. Simmer ½ hour over low heat.

Remove the meat from shells, add half to soup and save the remainder for garnish. Add cream to the soup and bring to a boil.

Puree in a blender and strain. Season with salt and pepper.

Garnish with reserved mussels and sprig of fresh thyme.

# Spicy Grilled Seabass with Peach Salsa

*Preparation Time: 45 Minutes*

**Four 7 oz. seabass fillets**
**1 tablespoon New Mexico chile powder**
**¼ teaspoon cinnamon**
**¼ teaspoon ground cumin**
**¼ teaspoon salt**
**⅛ teaspoon black pepper**
**2 oz. olive oil**
   **Juice from one lime**

Combine in a small bowl all spices, olive oil and lime juice. Remove the bones from the seabass fillets using tweezers or pliers. Coat the fish with the spice mixture and let sit ½ hour.

Grill the fish over hot charcoal for 2-3 minutes or until barely opaque, but do not overcook. Place the fish on warm plates and top with Peach Salsa. Serve immediately.

# Peach Salsa

*Preparation Time: 15 Minutes*

**2 ripe peaches, diced ¼ inch**
**1 green onion**
**½ lime**
**¼ red jalapeño, minced**
**2 sprigs mint, minced**
**1 tablespoon olive oil**

Dice the peaches and place in a bowl. Add the sliced green onion, red jalapeño, mint and juice from the lime. Toss together, combining well, add olive oil and toss to combine. Keep at room temperature until ready to serve.

# Sautéed Mushrooms with Young Lettuce and Goat Cheese

*Preparation Time: 25 Minutes*

6 oz. assorted wild mushrooms (chantrelles, woodear, shiitakes, oysters)
1 oz. goat cheese
8 oz. young lettuce (carugula, red oak, red mustard)
1 tablespoon extra virgin olive oil
¼ teaspoon fresh cracked black pepper

# Dressing

2 oz. balsamic vinaigrette
4 oz. extra virgin olive oil
   Salt
   Fresh cracked black pepper
1 teaspoon shallots, finely minced

Wash the mushrooms and remove tough stems. Sauté the mushrooms in olive oil, seasoning with salt and black pepper.

Toss the lettuce with dressing and divide onto 4 plates. Place the mushrooms on top of lettuce. Grate goat cheese on top of the mushrooms. Serve immediately.

# Grilled Vegetables

*Preparation Time: 15 Minutes*

**4 boiling onions, peeled**
**1 zucchini, cut crosswise into ¼ inch**
**1 red bell pepper, cut into ¼ inch**
**2 Japanese eggplant, cut in half, lengthwise**
**2 oz. olive oil**
**2 sprigs fresh thyme**
**1 clove garlic, finely minced**
  **Salt**
  **Fresh cracked black pepper**

Prepare the charcoal for grilling.

Combine the olive oil, thyme and garlic in a large bowl. Add the vegetables and toss gently to coat with oil. Season with salt and pepper.

Grill vegetables over hot coals until warm in the center and lightly browned on the outside.

# Terrine of Chocolate

*Preparation Time: 25 Minutes (note refrigeration time)*

12 oz. chocolate
4 oz. butter
3⅓ cup sugar
2 oz. sour cream
4 oz. cream
4 egg whites
4 egg yolks
**Garnish with whipped cream and strawberries**

Melt chocolate and butter together over double boiler. Beat the yolks and sugar together until they are light and creamy. Fold into the melted chocolate.

Whip the cream and sour cream together until stiff peaks form. Fold into the chocolate mixture.

Whip the egg whites until stiff peaks form. Fold the egg whites into the chocolate mix.

Place the chocolate mixture into a loaf pan, lined with waxed paper. Refrigerate for 4 hours.

Unmold and slice. Serve with whipped cream and strawberries.

# RAFFAELLO RESTAURANT

Mission between Ocean and 7th Ave.
Carmel, CA 93921
(408)624-1541

THIS INTIMATE AND elegant Northern Italian ristorante offers a true adventure in hospitality. Owner-chef Remo d'Agliano is dedicated to providing a dining experience second to none.

The superb cuisine, outstanding service and exceptional wine list offer a refined yet relaxing dining experience.

Buon appetito.

*Chef-owner Remo d'Agliano's Menu for Four*

*Fettuccine al Doppio Burro*
*Vitella Toscana*
*Chocolate Soufflé*

# Fettuccine al Doppio Burro

*Pre-heat oven to 350°*
*Preparation Time: 15 Minutes*

**1 lb. egg noodles**
**½ cup sweet butter**
**½ cup plus 2 tablespoons parmesan cheese, grated**
**¼ cup heavy cream**

Boil the noodles in salted water until al dente. Drain well.

Melt the butter and ½ cup parmesan cheese on low heat and pour over the cooked noodles. Add the cream and toss well.

Pour the noodle mixture into a buttered baking dish. Sprinkle the top with 2 tablespoons of parmesan cheese and bake at 350° for 10 minutes.

Serve hot and bubbly.

# Vitella Toscana

*Preparation Time: 45 Minutes*

4 veal chops
1 medium onion, sliced into rounds
1 oz. dried Porcini mushrooms
5 tomatoes, peeled and chopped
½ cup flour
3 tablespoons olive oil
2 tablespoons butter
½ cup dry white wine
   Salt and pepper to taste
1 lemon, sliced into rings

Sauté the onions in a large frying pan, using the olive oil and butter, until they are limp.

Flour the veal chops and add to the onions. Brown them well on both sides, adding salt and pepper to taste. Add the wine and lemon rings. When the wine has evaporated, remove the veal chops. Add the tomatoes and mushrooms to the sauce and cook on moderate heat for 15 minutes.

Put the veal chops back into the frying pan, cover and heat through until warm.

Serve immediately.

A suggested vegetable to accompany this meal is spinach, sautéed in butter or olive oil and garlic.

# Chocolate Soufflé

*Preparation Time: 20 Minutes*
*Pre-heat oven to 350°*
*Yields: 6 inch soufflé dish*

**3 oz. chocolate**
**¼ cup plus 1½ tablespoons granulated sugar**
**3 tablespoons milk**
**2 egg yolks**
**3 egg whites**
**¾ cup chocolate sauce**
  **Garnish with whipped cream or chocolate sauce**

In a double-boiler, melt the chocolate, sugar and the milk, beating until well mixed. Remove from the heat and allow it to cool for a few minutes. Add the egg yolks, beating constantly. Set aside.

Whip the egg whites until they are very stiff, adding 1½ tablespoons sugar halfway through. Fold the egg whites into the chocolate mixture.

Pour into a buttered and sugared soufflé mold. Bake 20 minutes at 350°.

Serve the soufflé with whipped cream or cool chocolate sauce.

# RIO GRILL

101 Crossroads Blvd.
Carmel, CA 93923
(408)625-5436

CREATIVE AMERICAN FOOD is well represented at the Rio Grill, where the freshest ingredients and oakwood smoker give the innovative appetizers and exciting entrees a wonderful flair.

What is there to eat? Start with the warm goat cheese, coated with almonds and nestled in a bed of endive and watercress, smothered with sun dried tomatoes, or the rabbit quesadilla with ancho chile and roasted tomatillo salsa. For the adventurous, how about a whole head of roasted garlic that has been bathed in olive oil and browned on the grill. Slice off the top and spread this outrageous mixture on sourdough bread. Exquisite! Fresh fish, herbed chicken, mustard-glazed duck and barbecued ribs pass through The Rio Grill's oak-burning oven-smoker.

The comfortable "Santa Fe" setting provides the perfect background for an intimate dinner or cocktails.

Like its sister restaurants, the Fog City Diner in San Francisco and Mustards in the Napa Valley, the Rio Grill is serious about food and fun.

## *Chef Sheila Marquez's Menu for Four*

*Roasted Garlic*
*Corn Salad with Steamed and Dressed Asparagus*
*Grilled Rabbit with Mustard Greens, Ginger and Sage*

# Roasted Garlic

*Preparation Time: 5 Minutes (note cooking time)*
*Pre-heat oven to 375°*

**1 large head of garlic**
**1 tablespoon olive oil**
   **Sliced sourdough bread or toast points**

Cut the top off the garlic and place root side down in a roasting pan. Sprinkle with olive oil and cover. Roast at 375° until soft. Approximately 60-90 minutes.

Slice the top off, so that the melted cloves can be scooped out and spread on sourdough bread or toast points.

# Corn Salad with Steamed and Dressed Asparagus

*Preparation Time: 15 Minutes*

½ lb. asparagus
 2 cups shucked sweet corn
 1 peeled avocado, sliced
 1 green onion, minced
½ cup rice vinegar
½ cup virgin olive oil
½ cup regular mild olive oil
 1 tablespoon mint, chopped
 1 tablespoon basil, chopped
    Salt and pepper to taste

Blanch the asparagus in hot water for 5 minutes or until tender when pricked with a fork. Let cool.

Combine ¼ cup rice vinegar and ¼ cup virgin olive oil and coat the asparagus. Set aside.

Mix the remaining vinegar, olive oil and herbs together. Season with salt and pepper. Mix in the corn, avocado and onion.

On a large platter, lay a strip of the corn salad at an angle across from the asparagus diagonally. Alternate with strips of corn salad and asparagus.

# Grilled Rabbit with Mustard Greens, Ginger and Sage

*Preparation Time: 45 Minutes (note elapsed time)*

 **2 rabbits**
 **¼ cup olive oil**
 **¼ bunch chopped thyme**
 **1 teaspoon white pepper**
 **¼ cup Dijon mustard**
 **1 cup white wine**
 **⅓ cup lemon juice**
 **¼ bunch sage**
 **1 inch peeled ginger, coarsely chopped**
 **2 shallots, chopped**
 **2 tablespoons cream**
 **1 lb. salted butter**
 **1 red onion, sliced**
 **4 shiitake mushrooms, sliced**
 **3 cups mustard greens, cut 1 inch wide**

Cut rabbits into 6 pieces. Front legs, back legs with thigh bone removed and boneless loin sections (saddles).

Combine olive oil, thyme, pepper and mustard. Marinate the rabbits for at least six hours.

Grill the front legs first (they take the longest), then back legs and saddle.

In a stainless saucepan over medium heat, combine white wine, lemon juice, sage, ginger and shallots for the sauce. Reduce all of these ingredients until dry. Add the cream and reduce by half. Build up with butter, a little at a time, whisking constantly over medium heat. Strain and add sage and ginger.

Just before serving, mix the onion, mushrooms and mustard greens. Place the rabbit over the greens and cover with the sauce.

# ROBATA GRILL AND SAKE BAR

3658 The Barnyard
Carmel, CA 93921
(408)624-2643

EXPERIENCE "OPEN HEARTH" cooking at this outstanding Japanese restaurant.

The menu offers an extensive list of appetizers from which you can put together a delicious dinner, as well as fresh mesquite grilled fish and unique dinner combinations.

The atmosphere is fun and authentic. The service is excellent.

The Robata Grill and Sake Bar is a delightful restaurant to savor a fine meal or enjoy a few drinks, in a distinctive setting.

grill and sake bar

### Chef Shigeo Yamane's Menu for Four

*Nikumaki (Filet Mignon Roll)*
*Shiitake Salmon*
*Yasai (Veggies) with Sesame Cream*
*Onigiri (BBQ Rice Ball)*

# Nikumaki

*Preparation Time: 45 Minutes*

**12 oz. thinly sliced filet mignon (sliced by butcher)**
**4 stalks of green onions**
**½ cup soy sauce**
**½ cup sugar**
**4 slices fresh ginger**
**3 oz. sake**
**Orange slice for garnish**

Combine soy sauce, sugar, ginger and sake in a heavy saucepan, over low heat until sugar is dissolved and ginger shrivels. Set aside.

Divide thin slices of filet mignon into four equal 3-oz. portions. Lay out the filets so each portion equals a 4"x6" rectangle.

Take one stalk of green onion and fold in half. Place on lower half of filet rectangle, then roll up to form sausage-like tube of filet with green onion in the center.

While forming Nikumaki, have your barbecue hot and ready for cooking. Cook to desired doneness. Remove from the fire and cut into one inch portions. Arrange on a small platter with a slice of orange, then dribble sauce over the Nikumaki and serve.

# Yasai with Sesame Cream

*Preparation Time: 15 Minutes*

**2 large carrots**
**2 green zucchinis**
**2 daikon**
**¼ lb. string beans**
**2 eggs**
**1 cup vegetable oil**
**1 tablespoon sesame oil**
**¼ cup soy sauce**
**2 garlic cloves, pressed**
**1 tablespoon rice vinegar**

Julienne all the vegetables to 3 inch long matchsticks.

Bring salted water to a boil and put the vegetables in the water for 1 minute and remove.

In a mixing bowl, with two egg yolks whisk the vegetable oil in very slowly, to emulsify. When the consistency is like mayonnaise, add the remaining ingredients and blend together.

Spoon on vegetables.

# Onigiri

**2 cups short grain rice**
**Sauce from Nikumaki**

Wash the rice and put it in a heavy pot. Cover with water ¾ inches above the level of the rice. Bring to a boil over high heat. Cover and reduce the heat to cook for 20 minutes. Let the rice cool after cooking.

Wet hands and form rice into thick hamburger patty. Brush with Nikumaki Sauce and grill on the barbecue until marked. Serve immediately.

# Shiitake Salmon

**4 salmon fillets, 8 oz. each**
**1 stalk green onion, chopped**
**½ cup vegetable oil**
**½ lb. shiitake mushrooms, sliced**
**1 tablespoon garlic, minced**
**1 tablespoon ginger, minced**
**2 tablespoons soy sauce**
   **Salt to taste**

Rub the salmon fillets with the vegetable oil and lightly salt. Place on barbecue.

Heat ¼ cup oil in a sauté pan over high heat, until light smoke appears. Add the mushrooms, garlic and ginger to cook for 20 seconds. Remove the pan from the heat and add the soy sauce.

Remove the grilled salmon from the barbecue. Top the salmon with the shiitake mushrooms and decorate with chopped green onions.

Fill the plates with fresh blanched vegetables and onigiri.

# SANS SOUCI

Lincoln between 5th & 6th Streets
P.O. Box 4805
Carmel, CA 93921
(408)624-6220

EXQUISITE CLASSIC FRENCH cuisine, a flickering fireplace, sparkling crystal chandeliers and brilliantly colored flower bouquets best describe Sans Souci—"without worry"—truly apropos.

Owned and operated by John and Cindy Kay Williams, Sans Souci has been in the family for 18 years, and their tradition for excellence is world renowned.

Chef Jean Hubert emphasizes the freshest foods available, such as roasted quail with pistachios, saddle of lamb with wild mushrooms and many of the fresh seafood specials.

One of the most romantic restaurants on the Peninsula.

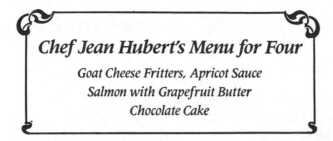

*Chef Jean Hubert's Menu for Four*

*Goat Cheese Fritters, Apricot Sauce*
*Salmon with Grapefruit Butter*
*Chocolate Cake*

# Goat Cheese Fritters, Apricot Sauce

*Preparation Time: 15 Minutes*

    1 lb. goat cheese
    2 cups peanut oil
    2 cups dark red port
   20 dried apricots
    2 cups flour
    1 egg
   12 oz. beer
       Pinch of sugar
       Salt and white pepper to taste
    1 bunch of watercress

In a mixing bowl combine the flour, egg, pinch of sugar and all but a sip of the beer. Mix well and let rest for ½ hour.

In a sauce pot place dried apricots and cover them with port, cooking over a low flame until apricots become soft and only half of the liquid surrounds them.

Form the goat cheese into 8 equal size balls and season them with salt and white pepper.

Begin to heat oil until it reaches 350° or until it is hot enough to fry quickly a test droplet of batter. Drop the goat cheese balls one at a time, first into batter then into hot oil. Cook approximately 1 minute or until they are crispy and golden brown.

On a warm platter pour apricots and their port syrup. Arrange the fritters on top and garnish with sprigs of fresh watercress.

# Salmon with Grapefruit Butter

*Preparation Time: 30 Minutes*

**2 lbs. salmon fillets (cut into 4 portions)**
**8 rubyred grapefruits, peeled and quartered**
**4 oz. sugar**
**2 oz. unsalted butter, cubed**
**½ oz. pink peppercorns**
**8 chives**

Season the salmon fillets and poach them 5 minutes over a low flame.

Combine 6 grapefruits and sugar in a sauce pot over medium heat until the juice has the consistency of a thick syrup. Add the butter, cube by cube, until it is completely incorporated into the juice. Season with salt and pepper.

Remove the salmon fillets from the stock, being sure to drain all excess liquid before placing them on a warm platter.

Pour the sauce over the salmon and garnish with the remaining 2 grapefruit sections, pink peppercorns and chives.

# Chocolate Cake

*Preparation Time: 30 Minutes*
*Pre-heat oven to 350°*

**4 cups sugar**
**8 egg yolks**
**8 egg whites**
**½ lb. cake flour, sifted**
**½ lb. unsalted butter, melted**
**3 oz. dark French style chocolate**

Whip the egg whites to firm peaks and set aside, keeping them cold.

Mix the yolks and sugar in a electric blender for 5 minutes or until yolks "ribbon". Slowly add all the flour, melted butter and melted chocolate. Fold in the egg whites.

Pour into a floured 10" cake pan and bake for 10-15 minutes at 350°. The cake is done when a toothpick comes out dry after being inserted in the middle of the cake. Cool on a rack.

# Frosting

**3 egg yolks**
**3 egg whites**
**¼ lb. unsalted butter, cubed**
**⅛ cup hot cream**
**½ lb. dark chocolate**

Add the melted chocolate to the egg yolks and blend in the hot cream. Slowly add the butter cubes one at a time until completely blended.

Whip egg whites until firm and fold into the chocolate mixture.

Pour the frosting over the cooled cake. Chill both and serve with whipped cream and fresh fruit garnish.

# CARMEL VALLEY: RURAL ROOTS

WITHOUT THE PRECIOUS water of the Carmel River, the Monterey Peninsula could not have grown.

The Pacific Improvement Company, owned by the Big Four of railroad fame, needed a large supply of water for its Hotel Del Monte. The massive resort hotel contained hundreds of guest rooms and featured the Roman Plunge, an immense swimming pool.

About 700 Chinese laborers were hired to build the original San Clemente Dam and to lay twelve-inch pipe to bring the water out of the valley.

Because of the ready availability of water and its fertile soil, Carmel Valley became an agricultural and cattle center. Today, the cowboy character of the early valley remains, mingling with upscale homes, lush golf courses, posh resorts, tennis clubs, fruit orchards, and sprawling shopping complexes at its mouth.

LARGE TRACTS OF LAND were granted by Mexico after its freedom from Spain in 1822. After the end of the U.S.-Mexican War in 1848, the land grants had to be confirmed by a California board.

Four land grants involved Carmel Valley. Canada de la Segunda, 4,366 acres near the entrance to the valley, were granted in 1836 to Lazaro Soto; the grant was confirmed to Andrew Randall et al in 1858. El Potrero de San Carlos, 4,306 acres, was granted to Fructuoso (no first name given) in 1837; the grant was confirmed in 1855 to Joaquin Gutierez and patented in 1862. Los Laureles, 6,624 acres, was granted to J.M. Boronda in 1839; the grant was confirmed to Boronda in 1856. Los Tularcitos, 26,581 acres in upper Carmel Valley, extending up Chupines Creek toward Tassajara Hot Springs, was granted in 1834 to Rafael Gomez; the grant was confirmed to his heirs in 1855.

THE SHELTERED VALLEY boasts temperatures 10 to 20° higher than the foggier coastal regions. Verdant meadows and a profusion of spring wildflowers nestle between oak-dotted mountains.

The valley stretches for about 26 miles from Highway 1 to the Jamesburg area. A wonderful place for a leisurely drive, the eastern end of the valley leads to the large Salinas Valley, its inland highways and enormous fields.

The farther one travels east along Carmel Valley Road, the easy-going rural atmosphere becomes more apparent. As the golf courses are left behind, the roads get curvier and the scenery becomes more unspoiled. Deep into the valley, cowboys' dented pickup trucks and expensive European sedans are more likely to share the roads.

OF PARTICULAR importance to the dining experience on the Monterey Peninsula are the exotic vegetables and herbs cultivated in Carmel Valley.

Carmel Valley contains some of the most whimsical street names in the county. Camino de Quien Sabe is Spanish for Street of Who Knows. The mellifluous Salsipuedes means Get Out If You Can.

The mouth of Carmel Valley, adjacent to Highway 1, features artichoke fields and two large shopping complexes, the Barnyard and the Crossroads. Each specializes in chic boutiques, specialty shops, a scattered array of restaurants, art galleries and masses of decorative flowers.

CARMEL VALLEY DATEBOOK: Fiesta de los Amigos, April; Carmel Valley Ranchers' Day, September.

# THE COVEY RESTAURANT

Quail Lodge
8205 Valley Greens Drive
Carmel, CA 93923
(408)624-1581

IN A PEACEFUL country setting, minutes from Carmel, the Covey Restaurant is nestled among lavish golf fairways, a lake and landscaped grounds. Continental cuisine with a California touch is served by the lake, offering panoramic picture-window views of the lighted fountain and bridge.

Chef Bob Williamson combines quality with simplicity in his progressive creations.

Quail Lodge is perhaps best known as one of the very few Mobil 5 Star establishments in the United States, the only one between San Francisco and Los Angeles.

The resort conveys casual elegance with a passion for quality.

QUAIL LODGE

*Chef Bob Williamson's Menu for Eight*

*Leek and Onion Soup with Fresh Horseradish Cream*
*Roulade of Sole and Salmon in a Paprika Sauce*
*Dilled Cucumbers*
*Chicken Stuffed with Dates, Ham and Walnuts*
*Cranberry Glaze*
*Wild Rice*
*Chocolate and Grand Marnier Mousse Torte*

# Leek and Onion Soup with Fresh Horseradish Cream

*Preparation Time: 30 Minutes*

**2 tablespoons butter**
**2 small leeks**
**1 medium onion, diced**
**2 small boiling onions, cut into rings**
**2 sprigs thyme (or ½ teaspoon dried thyme)**
**3 quarts chicken broth**
**⅔ cup horseradish, scraped (or 2 tablespoons prepared**
    **horseradish)**
**1 cup whipping cream**
    **Salt and white pepper to taste.**

Cut off the bottom third of the leeks and cut them across in regular slices about ³⁄₁₆". Wash well in cold water, separating the "rings" in the process and chop.

Place the butter, chopped leeks, chopped onion and thyme in a heavy saucepan and sauté over moderate heat without coloring, approximately 3-6 minutes. Add the chicken broth. Bring to a boil and simmer 15 minutes. Add the boiling onions, bringing the mixture back to a boil. Simmer for 5 minutes. Season to taste with salt and pepper.

Whip the cream and gently fold in the horseradish.

Serve the soup in bowls and pass the horseradish cream separately.

# Halibut and Salmon Roulade

*Preparation Time: 30 Minutes*

12 oz. halibut fillet
12 oz. salmon fillet
½ teaspoon dill, chopped
1 cup flour
3 tablespoons clarified butter
Salt and white pepper to taste

Thinly slice the halibut and arrange the slices to form a rectangle 10″ × 8″ on a well-buttered parchment paper. Cover it with plastic wrap. Roll it gently with a rolling pin to form an even layer. Remove the wrap and sprinkle halibut with chopped dill. Season lightly with salt and pepper.

Thinly slice the salmon and arrange the slices on top of the halibut. Cover with wrap and roll again, very gently.

Remove the wrap, using the parchment paper to assist, and roll the fish to form a long roll. Wrapped in parchment, trim off the excess paper. Cut the roll into eight even pieces. Dust the exposed fish with flour.

Using a thick-bottomed 12″ sauté pan, heat the clarified butter until it forms a light haze. Stand the rings of fish in the pan and cook over moderate heat for 4 minutes each side, turning once.

Remove from the pan and peel off the parchment paper. Serve the roulade on the paprika sauce, garnished with the dilled cucumber.

# Paprika Sauce

*Preparation Time: 15 Minutes*

**2 strips bacon, diced**
**2 shallots, chopped**
**1 small carrot, chopped**
**1 rib celery, chopped**
**2 large tomatoes, chopped**
**1 bay leaf**
**1 sprig marjoram (or ¼ teaspoon dried)**
**2 tablespoons sweet paprika**
**2 cups clam juice**
**1 cup sour cream**
**2 tablespoons flour**
**½ tablespoon lemon juice**
   **Salt and pepper to taste**

Place the bacon in a two quart saucepan and heat gently until the bacon starts to crisp, approximately 3-4 minutes.

Add the shallots, carrot, celery, bay leaf and marjoram. Cover the pan and sauté the vegetables on moderate heat for 3-4 minutes without coloring. Remove from the heat and mix in the paprika. Add the tomato and clam juice. Return to the heat and bring to a boil. Cover and simmer for 15 minutes.

Mix the flour and sour cream together and whisk into the simmering liquid. Season with salt and pepper to taste. Add the lemon juice and cook 5 minutes. Strain.

For a richer sauce incorporate 2-3 tablespoons unsalted butter.

# Dilled Cucumbers

*Preparation Time: 15 Minutes*

1 medium English cucumber
2 tablespoons butter
½ teaspoon sugar
¼ cup white wine
1 teaspoon chopped dill
   Salt and pepper to taste

    Cut the cucumber lengthwise into four even pieces. Remove the seeds. Make a strip along the outside of each piece with a peeler. Cut the cucumbers crosswise into 4 sections with a small knife and shape each piece into a long oval.

    Heat a 10″ skillet and add the butter and cucumber. Add the sugar and toss the cucumbers until they are shiny. Add the wine and dill. Cover and cook gently until the cucumbers soften slightly, 3-4 minutes. Remove the lid and evaporate the remaining liquid over high heat, constantly tossing the cucumbers. Season lightly with salt.

    Use the dill cucumbers to garnish the roulade.

# Chicken with Date and Walnut Stuffing

*Preparation Time: One Hour (note stock cooking time)*

**Four 4 lb. large frying chickens or range hens**
  **2 ribs of celery**
  **1 leek**
  **1 medium onion**
  **2 bay leaves**
  **2 sprigs thyme (or ¼ teaspoon dried thyme)**
**1-inch piece ginger root**
**1¼ gallon water**
  **3 tablespoons clarified butter**

Remove the legs from the hens and reserve for another use. Cut the winglets off, just inside the second joint. Pull the skin off. Remove the wishbone and cut off the breasts, leaving the wing bone attached to the breast. Refrigerate breasts while you prepare the stock, sauce and stuffing.

# Stock

Make a chicken stock with the carcass, winglets and trimmings by placing them in a stew pan with assorted seasonal vegetables, water and aromatics. Bring the mixture to a boil and simmer 2½ hours. Strain and skim. Reduce liquid to approximately 1 cup.

# Sauce

4 cups cranberries
2 tablespoons sugar (or more to taste)
2 cups water
3 tablespoons butter, unsalted
1 tablespoon arrowroot in 2 tablespoons water
1 cup reduced chicken stock
   Salt and pepper to taste

Boil the cranberries, water and sugar together until the fruit is soft. Strain. Reduce the liquid to approximately 1 cup.

Add the reduced chicken stock. Thicken with the arrowroot. Whisk in the unsalted butter.

Season to taste with salt and pepper.

# Wild Rice

1 cup wild rice
2 cups water
   Salt to taste

After briefly rinsing rice under tap water, bring the ingredients to a boil. Cover and simmer for 40 minutes. Do not remove the lid. Turn off the heat, and allow to set, covered, a few more minutes. Fluff prior to serving.

# Stuffing

**1 cup pitted dates (4 oz.) coarsely chopped**
**⅔ cup walnuts**
**1 tablespoon shallots, chopped**
**2 tablespoons parsley, chopped**
**½ cup ham, chopped**
**⅔ cup white breadcrumbs**
**⅛ teaspoon ground black pepper**

Place all ingredients except the breadcrumbs in a food processor and blend together in short "pulses". DO NOT OVERPROCESS. Blend in the breadcrumbs.

Place the chicken breasts skin side down on the cuttingboard. Lift the "tenderloin" or fillets from each breast. Flatten the breasts and fillets with a meat mallet.

Put some of the stuffing on each breast. Cover it with the fillets and fold over the breast meat to form a nice thin "package". Season with salt and pepper and dust with flour.

Heat 3 tablespoons clarified butter in a heavy flat sauté pan. Place the breasts, folded side down in the pan. This will seal the closure.

To serve, put the wild rice in the center of each plate and surround it with the cranberry sauce. Place a chicken breast on top of the rice.

# Chocolate and Grand Marnier Mousse Torte

*Preparation Time: 45 Minutes (note refrigeration time)*
*Serves 12*

**4 cups soft cake crumbs**
**2 teaspoons orange zest**
**4 tablespoons clarified butter**
**2 tablespoons Grand Marnier**

Mix the ingredients together and press evenly onto the bottom of a 12" tart pan with a removable base. Set aside.

# Mousse

**12 oz. Swiss chocolate couverture**
**⅓ cup water**
**⅔ cup sugar**
**5 egg yolks**
**3 egg whites**
**1½ cups whipping cream**
**⅓ cup strong coffee**
**3 tablespoons Grand Marnier**
**3 oz. soft butter (unsalted)**

Slowly melt the couverture over a double boiler, taking care that it does not get wet.

Boil the water and sugar together for 3 minutes. Add the butter, egg yolks, coffee and Grand Marnier and cook carefully until it thickens to a creamy consistency. Remove from the heat.

Add the melted couverture and whisk in. Whip the egg whites and fold in. Whip the cream and fold in.

Pour the mousse into the tart pan and chill one hour.

Run a small hot knife around the edge of the tart pan to loosen from the mold. Smooth the edges of the mousse with a hot palette knife. Chill while you prepare the frosting.

# Frosting

**12 oz. Swiss chocolate couverture**
**1½ cups cream**
 **½ cup strong coffee**
 **2 tablespoons Grand Marnier**
 **½ cup soft butter**

Finely chop the chocolate. Boil the cream and coffee together. Remove from heat and add the chocolate. Work well with a wooden spoon until the chocolate is fully blended. Add the Grand Marnier.

Remove from the heat and whisk in the soft butter. Let the mixture cool before using a pastry bag to decorate the torte.

# THE RIDGE RESTAURANT

Robles del Rio Lodge
200 Punta Del Monte
Carmel Valley, CA 93924
(408)659-2264

DINING IS A GOURMET'S delight at The Ridge. Chef Daniel Barduzzi reflects both his intense training in classical French cuisine and an artistic inspiration for pleasing the contemporary California palate.

He uses the freshest ingredients from Monterey County harvests. Libations are available in the cantina.

Robles del Rio Lodge was built in the late 1920's, perched on top of a mountain surrounded by oak trees. The guest rooms range from a board-and-battened countryside look to a Laura Ashley motif.

An exceptional dining and lodging experience in a homey and tranquil setting.

*Chef Daniel Barduzzi's Menu for Four*

*Scallops in Fresh Basil and Tomato*
*Monterey Fish Soup*
*Cornish Game Hen Carmel Valley*

# Scallops in Fresh Basil and Tomato

*Preparation Time: 25 Minutes*

**24 scallops**
**2 medium size ripe tomatoes**
**2 garlic cloves, peeled**
**½ bunch fresh basil, stems removed**
**1 tablespoon olive oil**
**2 oz. butter**
**1 tablespoon vegetable oil**
**Chopped Italian parsley for garnish**
**Salt and pepper to taste**

Rinse and drain the scallops and dry them on a towel.

Quickly blanch the tomatoes in simmering water for 1 minute and remove to ice water. Seed and dice the tomatoes.

In a food processor combine the tomatoes, basil, garlic and olive oil and blend to a coarse mixture. Set aside.

Dust scallops in flour. In a sauté pan add the vegetable oil and butter over high heat until the butter starts to brown. Add the scallops and sauté very quickly and briefly. Remove from the pan and keep warm on the side.

Without washing the pan, remove any excess oils, and add the tomato and basil mixture. Sauté briefly, adding salt and pepper. Add the scallops and garnish with parsley.

# Monterey Fish Soup

*Preparation Time: One Hour*

1½ lb. fillet of red snapper
  1 leek stalk, diced
  1 medium onion, diced
  2 carrots, diced
  1 celery stalk, diced
  12 French bread croutons
  10 oz. grated Swiss cheese
  1 teaspoon fennel
  1 teaspoon oregano
  1 teaspoon thyme
  3 garlic cloves
  3 tablespoons olive oil
  4 tablespoons tomato puree
  1 cup Monterey Chardonnay
  1 quart water
    Salt and pepper to taste

In a soup pot, heat the olive oil over medium heat. Add 2 crushed garlic cloves, onions, carrots, celery, leek and fennel. Stir well and cover for 2 minutes. Add the red snapper, stir and cover again for 2 minutes. Mix in the tomato puree, oregano and thyme, and again cover for 2 minutes. Add Chardonnay, water, salt and pepper and bring to a boil. Reduce heat to simmer for 40 minutes.

Remove from the heat and puree with a food mill.

Serve with a side garnish of grated cheese and toasted croutons that have been rubbed with the last garlic clove.

# Cornish Game Hen Carmel Valley

*Preparation Time: One Hour*
*Pre-heat oven to 400°*

**Two 20 oz. Cornish game hens**
  **½ lb. sausage meat**
 **10 oz. whole chestnuts in water, diced (keep 5 for garnish)**
  **1 small onion, finely chopped**
  **1 celery stick, diced**
  **1 carrot, sliced in eighths**
  **2 teaspoons chopped parsley**
  **1 oz. brandy**
  **3 oz. dry white wine**
  **1 egg**
  **1 oz. oil**
  **2 teaspoons butter**
    **Salt, pepper and thyme to taste**

In a sauté pan with 1 oz. of oil, cook the sausage meat, stirring constantly for 10 minutes or until most of the fat is dissolved. Remove the fat and let the sausage cool for 30 minutes.

Add the onion, chestnuts, celery, parsley, brandy, egg and thyme to the sausage and mix well. Do not add salt and pepper.

Stuff the birds with the sausage mixture and tie their legs to keep the stuffing inside. Sauté the hens in 1 oz. of oil over medium heat, until they are a gold color. Put them on their backs in a baking pan and add 1 teaspoon of butter, the onion and carrot. Bake for 40 minutes at 400°.

When cooked, remove the birds from the sauté pan, but leave the carrot and onions in. Deglace the pan with white wine and equal amount of water, bringing the sauce to a boil. Reduce by half. Salt and pepper to taste.

In a separate pan, sauté the remaining chestnuts in 1 teaspoon of butter, to warm them.

Spoon sauce and vegetables over the hens and garnish with the sautéed chestnuts.

# BIG SUR:
# SEACOAST SUPREME

THE STUNNING BEAUTY of Big Sur extends 75 miles from Point Lobos, just south to Carmel, to Santa Lucia, just north of the Hearst Castle at San Simeon.

That stretch along Highway 1 includes spectacular ocean vistas from the cliff-hugging road, redwoods creeping toward the coast, isolated beaches and coves where the roaring surf is one's only companion, lush state parks, a world-class spa, and exquisite homes tucked against the monumental cliffs.

Romantic couples who draw inspiration from being isolated amid stunning surroundings would be well advised to pause and relish the Big Sur coast.

POINT LOBOS, a state reserve just south of Carmel, is a great place to explore tide pools, watch whales from the cliffs, stroll paths that curl around twisted Monterey cypresses, spy on colonies of sea otters, and listen to the choirs of sea lions that congregate on the offshore rocks. Whaler's Cove, site of an old whaling station (a cabin on the shore has floor joists made out of whale ribs), is now a scuba-diving paradise. The languid inlet also boasts a history of shipwrecks, gold mining, smuggling, and was the site of an abalone cannery.

SCHOLARS SAY that Robert Louis Stevenson used the rugged coast of Point Lobos as the model for Treasure Island.

The Coast Highway was the brainchild of Dr. John Roberts, the physician on horseback who traversed the pack horse trail to Big Sur in order to bring medical services to the remote residents.

DR. ROBERTS in 1915 convinced the state legislature that a highway should be carved along the cliffs. With much of the labor performed by prison convicts, the road was completed in 1937. At the opening ceremonies, a proud Dr. Roberts called it "without a doubt the most spectacular and awe-inspiring scenic highway in the United States, perhaps the world."

Palo Colorado Canyon contains a twisting, sun-speckled road that meanders around coastal redwood trees. An impressive side trip, the canyon takes the visitor to a quiet world of cool ferns and giant trees. Be sure you take your time driving the road; it's narrow and curvy, but worth the leisurely trip.

BIXBY CREEK BRIDGE, originally known as the Rainbow Bridge, is one of the world's highest single span concrete bridges: it's over 260 feet high and over 700 feet long. The graceful bridge seldom fails to lure photographers.

Pfeiffer Big Sur State Park marks the location of the first inn in Big Sur. Pioneer Florence Pfeiffer grew tired of putting up adventuresome travelers in her home for free. So, in the early 1900s, she started charging $1 for dinner, bed and breakfast. An extra 50 cents took care of stabling and feeding each horse.

It is said that actor Orson Welles bought the site of Nepenthe for sexy film siren Rita Hayworth. It is doubtful she ever took possession of the wonderful property, but it has flourished ever since.

THE ESALEN SPA got its start with an old Indian telling tales of a miraculous spring along the coast. Tom Slate, a young man crippled with arthritis, was transported over the difficult trail to the hot mineral baths. Slate was cured, so he bought the springs and surrounding acreage and Esalen was born.

The Big Sur Marathon, held in May, pits long-distance runners against the ups and downs of the Coast Highway. The finish line is at Rio Road, at the mouth of Carmel Valley.

BIG SUR DATEBOOK: Big Sur Marathon, May; Big Sur River Run, October.

# CAFE AMPHORA

Highway 1 at Nepenthe
Big Sur, CA 93920
(408)667-2660

PERCHED STRATEGICALLY on a bluff overlooking the powerful Pacific with a 50 mile view of the breathtaking Big Sur Coast is Cafe Amphora.

A wide variety of eggs benedict, omelettes, sandwiches, fabulous homemade desserts and beer and wine are served on a large, flower-filled terrace 850 feet above the ocean.

Cafe Amphora is open 10—5 p.m. daily, weather permitting.

*Owner-Chef Robin Burnside's Menu for Four*

*The California Benedict*
*Cafe Salsa*
*Walnut Pie*

# Cafe Salsa

*Preparation Time: 15 Minutes*

1 bunch cilantro
12 roma tomatoes
5 tomatillos
1 small red onion
10 cloves garlic
2 jalapeño peppers
4 serrano peppers
    Juice of one lime
    Juice of one lemon
    Juice of one orange
    Salt to taste

In a food processor or blender blend the tomatillos, garlic, both peppers with the citrus juices and salt.

Finely chop the cilantro, tomatoes and red onion and mix with the pepper mixture.

Serve with blue corn tortilla chips.

# The California Benedict

*Preparation Time: 15 Minutes*

**2 egg yolks**
  **Juice of one lime**
**1 lb. clarified sweet butter**
  **A few dashes hot sauce (our favorite brand is Sirachi, from Thailand)**
**4 toasted whole wheat English muffins**
**8 poached eggs**
  **California Varieties: sautéed mushrooms, sautéed turkey, sautéed ham, avocado, sautéed sliced tomatoes with salsa, smoked salmon.**

In a blender add the egg yolks, lime juice and hot sauce. With the blender on high, slowly pour in the butter. Add drops of warm water as needed to maintain blending.

Place the English muffins on a plate with the chosen variety, or combinations of the California varieties. Nest the poached eggs on the muffins and top with the hollandaise sauce.

Garnish the plate with sliced fresh fruit.

# Walnut Pie

*Preparation Time: 1½ Hours*
*Pre-heat oven to 350°*

# Pie Dough

¼ cup sweet butter
1 cup flour
1½ tablespoon sugar
2 tablespoons water

Blend the flour, sugar and butter into a coarse meal. Slowly add the water to the mixture and form into a ball. Roll the dough out and place in a pie plate with high fluted edges. Chill.

# Filling

2 tablespoons butter
½ lb. brown sugar
¼ cup white sugar
5 eggs
1½ cups dark corn syrup
1 tablespoon vanilla
1½ cups walnuts, chopped

Cream together the butter, brown sugar and white sugar until smooth. Add the eggs, one at a time and mix until light. Add the corn syrup and vanilla and mix well.

Pour into a pie shell and sprinkle with walnuts, pressing lightly into the filling.

Bake at 350° for approximately one hour or until set. (Pie will begin to crack). Cool to room temperature before serving. This pie freezes well.

# DEETJEN'S BIG SUR INN

Highway 1
P.O. Box 80
Big Sur, CA 93920
(408) 667-2377

THIS CHARMING RURAL inn, whose warm hospitality typifies a lighthearted and casual atmosphere, is located among massive redwood and pine trees in Big Sur.

Guests come to this rustic inn, built in the 1930's, to get away from it all, to enjoy the peace and quiet of the setting, and to regenerate their spirit.

Deetjen's offers 20 rooms with a restaurant serving breakfast and dinner, with homey comfort and history in equal measure.

*Chef John Redfield's Menu for Four*

*Baked Artichoke Hearts*
*Seafood Curry*
*Pavlova*

# Baked Artichoke Hearts

*Preparation Time: 20 Minutes*
*Pre-heat oven to 500°*

 **6 large artichoke hearts**
**½ cup Swiss cheese, grated**
 **1 cup white wine**
 **4 teaspoons sour cream**
    **Sliced tomatoes**

Steam the artichoke hearts and slice ¼ inch thick.

Place the artichokes in a 4-6 oz. baking dish. Cover with the cheese and pour the white wine over the cheese.

Bake for 10 minutes at 500°. Top with sour cream and sliced tomatoes.

# Seafood Curry

*Preparation Time: 25 Minutes*

**Four 5 oz. fillets of sole**
**12 oz. bay scallops**
**16-20 large prawns**
  **½ cup white wine**
   **1 teaspoon ginger, finely grated**
   **1 teaspoon garlic, finely grated**
   **3 tablespoons curry powder**
   **1 medium onion, sliced**
   **1 large bell pepper, sliced**
 **12 mushrooms, diced**
   **2 tomatoes, sliced in eighths**
   **1 cup snow peas**
    **Juice of ½ lemon**

Clean and devein the prawns and set aside.

In a saucepan over medium heat combine wine, ginger, garlic and curry. When the sauce is hot, add the seafood, onions, pepper, mushrooms, tomatoes and snow peas. Stir quickly. Add the lemon juice and cook for 7-10 minutes, stirring constantly.

Serve the Seafood Curry with rice.

# Pavlova

*Preparation Time: 2½ Hours*
*Pre-heat oven to 275°*

4 egg whites
1 teaspoon malt vinegar
1 teaspoon pure vanilla extract
¼ teaspoon salt
1 cup fine sugar
1 tablespoon cornstarch
2 pints of whipped cream
    Fresh fruit of raspberries, kiwi, strawberries or cherries.

Beat the egg whites with salt and malt vinegar until they are very stiff. Add the ½ cup sugar to the egg whites and beat well. Fold in the rest of the sugar, cornstarch and vanilla.

Gently transfer the mixture to a 8″ circle on an oiled cooking sheet. Shape evenly, 2-3 inches deep, in a smooth circle.

Bake on the lowest shelf of the oven for two hours at 275°. Let cool. (The top will crack during the cooling process).

Top with whipped cream and decorate with fresh fruits of your choice. Cut gently with a hot knife.

# VENTANA

Big Sur, CA
93920
(408)624-4812

DINE A THOUSAND feet above the Pacific in Ventana's elegantly appointed restaurant, where windows reveal a dramatic expanse of ocean and mountains.

The award-winning menu offers exceptional luncheons and dinners every day of the year, in an atmosphere of airy natural cedar and fireside warmth or on the beautifully landscaped terrace. The romance of view and food make it one of the world's great dining experiences.

The inn is a retreat for discriminating lovers. The high ceilings, fireplaces, ocean view balconies, saunas and Japanese hot baths make this country inn an unusually romantic and spectacularly beautiful place to be.

*Chef Tom Grego's Menu for Four*

*Fettucine with Oyster and Shiitake Mushrooms in Brown Butter*
*Tomatillo Anaheim Chile Soup*
*Warm Pear Salad with Butter Lettuce*
*Grilled Filet Mignon with Roasted Garlic Sauce and Balsamic Vinegar*
*Chocolate Torte*

# Fettucine with Oyster and Shiitake Mushrooms in Brown Butter

*Preparation Time: 25 Minutes*

8 oz. butter
1½ oz. shallots, minced
½ oz. garlic, minced
4 oz. oyster mushrooms, sliced
4 oz. shiitake mushrooms, stems removed, sliced
1 tablespoon lemon juice
2 oz. romano cheese, grated
10 oz. fresh fettucine

Melt the butter in a saucepan until brown. Skim the foam and pour the brown butter into the sauté pan, leaving the sediment behind.

Sauté the shallots and garlic in the brown butter for two minutes. Add the mushrooms and sauté for 5 minutes. Add the lemon juice and season to taste.

Divide the sauce over the cooked pasta and sprinkle with the romano cheese.

# Tomatillo Anaheim Chile Soup

*Preparation Time: 35 Minutes*

10 Anaheim chiles
 2 gallons veal stock
 ½ cup bacon drippings
 1 fresh garlic bulb, pureed
 6 onions, diced
 ½ oz. chile powder
 ½ oz. cumin
 ½ bunch cilantro, chopped
 1 cup brandy
 5 lbs. tomatillos, diced
 ½ quart heavy cream
    Salt and pepper to taste

Roast the chiles over an open fire, seed and core them.

In a blender or food processor, puree the chiles in the veal stock. Strain, and discard the remaining skins.

In a soup pot, heat the bacon drippings with the garlic. Briefly sauté the onions and spices. Add the brandy and cook for one minute. Add the pureed chiles and veal stock, tomatillos and cilantro, bringing the mixture to a boil. Simmer for 20 minutes.

Puree the soup and add the cream. Salt and pepper to taste.

# Warm Pear Salad with Butter Lettuce

*Preparation Time: 25 Minutes*
*Pre-heat oven to 350°*

  4 pears
16 oz. port
  4 oz. walnuts, chopped
  4 oz. stilton cheese
  2 heads butter lettuce, cleaned and leaves separated

Cut the pears in half and poach in the port until soft, approximately 15 minutes. Scoop out the center of the pears.

Mix the walnuts and cheese together and mound in the pears. Bake at 350° for 5 minutes or until the cheese starts to melt.

Place on a bed of butter lettuce which has been tossed in the vinaigrette.

# Vinaigrette

8 oz. walnut oil
2 oz. pear vinegar
1 oz. shallot, minced
   Salt and pepper to taste

Place in a jar and shake well.

# Grilled Filet Mignon with Roasted Garlic Sauce and Balsamic Vinegar

*Preparation Time: 45 Minutes*
*Pre-heat oven to 350°*

1 garlic bulb
1 tablespoon olive oil
1 cup brown sauce
2 oz. heavy cream
1 teaspoon balsamic vinegar

Remove the individual cloves of garlic, leaving the skin intact. Place in a sauté pan and drizzle with olive oil.

Roast in a 350° oven for 20-25 minutes until soft. When cool enough to handle, squeeze the garlic out of the skins into a sauce pan. Add the brown sauce and simmer for 10 minutes.

Puree the garlic and brown sauce in a blender. Return to the sauce pan and add the vinegar, cream, salt and pepper. Simmer until the sauce coats the back of a spoon. Pass through a wire strainer.

Grill the filet to your desired doneness. Spoon the sauce on a plate, placing the filet on top.

# Chocolate Torte

*Preparation Time: 45 Minutes (note elapsed time)*
*Pre-heat oven to 375°*

1 cup butter
1 cup sugar
5 eggs, separated
4 tablespoons arrowroot or ½ cup flour
3 oz. unsweetened chocolate
3 oz. semisweet chocolate
4 tablespoons brandy
2 teaspoons vanilla
   Nuts or chocolate vermicelle garnish

    Melt the chocolate and let cool. Cream the butter, adding ¾ cup of the sugar until fluffy. Add the egg yolks one at a time. Add the sifted arrowroot or flour. Add the cooled chocolate, vanilla and brandy.
    Beat the whites to a soft peak. Fold into the chocolate mixture.
    Bake at 375° for 30 minutes or more (the center should be soft) and let cool. Turn upside down and let sit overnight.

# Glaze

6 oz. semisweet chocolate
2 tablespoons butter
¼ cup cream

    Melt all the ingredients on low heat. Spread designing patterns on the torte. Press the nuts or chocolate vermicelle around the sides.

# MONTEREY COUNTY WINES:
# A PLEASANT SURPRISE

FRANCISCAN FRIARS planted the county's first wine grapes almost 200 years ago in the Spanish mission at Soledad.

But it took until 1960 for Monterey County to realize its full potential as a wine-producing region, when established wineries such as Chalone, Wente, Mirassou and Paul Masson expanded their plantings to the county. Now, Monterey contains 35,000 acres of grapes.

The county's vintners tend to favor varietals that consistently yield good to superior wines. Among the outstanding varieties with dozens of medals in state and national competitions are Cabernet Sauvignon, Chardonnay, Pinot Noir, Johannisberg Riesling, Pinot Blanc, Chenin Blanc, Gewurztraminer and Champagne.

OTHER REGIONS of the state may still be better known for their wines, but fine wines with the Monterey appellation are reaping widespread praise. Monterey County wines display distinctive qualities, including unusual fruitiness, well-developed color and good sugar-acid balance.

The growing success of the county's wines is attributed to three key elements: near-perfect climate, fertile soil and a solid blend of traditional and scientific methods used by growers and winemakers.

In addition, some of the more select wineries tend to take greater care in producing smaller volumes of distinctive wines.

We encourage you to savor Monterey County wines. You may be very pleasantly surprised.

# Monterey County

# Wine Regions

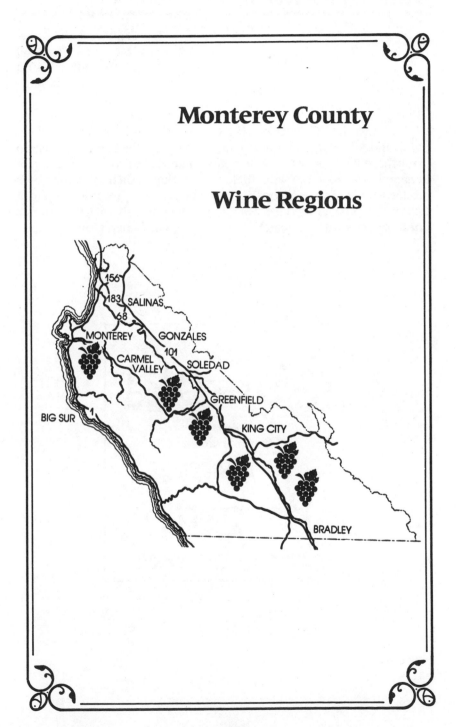

# BARGETTO WINERY

700 Cannery Row Suite L
Monterey, CA 93940
(408)373-4053
Open daily

THE BARGETTO WINERY was founded in 1933 by brothers Philip and John Bargetto who had emigrated from the Piedmonte region of northern Italy. Today, the winery is operated by the third generation of Bargettos, who have the same lifelong ambition as their forefathers—to produce wines of superior quality. Bargetto is not ony regarded as one of California's premier producers of fine varietals, but also of the country's finest natural fruit wines such as Raspberry, Olallieberry and Apricot.

1986
Central Coast
White Riesling

Bargetto

PRODUCED AND BOTTLED BY BARGETTO'S SANTA CRUZ WINERY
SOQUEL, CALIFORNIA. ALCOHOL 11.7% BY VOLUME

# Shrimp in Riesling/Dijon Sauce

*Preparation Time: 15 Minutes*
*Serves 4*

3 tablespoons olive oil
3 tablespoons butter
4 large cloves garlic, cut in half
1 cup Bargetto White Riesling
2 tablespoons Dijon style mustard
2 lbs. shrimp, shelled and deveined

In a large, heavy skillet, heat oil and butter until haze forms. Add garlic and cook until browned. Remove garlic and discard. Add wine and bring to a boil. Lower heat and whisk in mustard. Add shrimp and cook until shrimp are pink (3 to 4 minutes). Serve with lots of sourdough bread for dunking in the sauce and, of course, drink the rest of the Riesling with the shrimp.

# Raspberry Salad Dressing

*Preparation Time: 10 Minutes*

1 tablespoon blue cheese
2 tablespoons Raspberry Wine
2 tablespoons Chef Luigi Wine Vinegar
2 tablespoons almond pieces
½ cup olive oil

Blend the first four ingredients until smooth. Add the olive oil slowly until the mixture is emulsified.

# CHALONE VINEYARD

P.O. Box 855
Soledad, CA 93960
Telephone Orders (415)546-7755
Winery tours by appointment

CHALONE VINEYARD IS remotely situated in the Gavilan Mountains to the east of the Salinas Valley. Here they produce small lots of 100% varietal Estate Bottled wines from grapes grown on the property.

The vines at Chalone Vineyard must cope with an extremely dry climate and a sparse limestone soil. The sheer difficulty of growing grapes here makes one pause. The obstacles include deer, rabbits, gophers, birds, and low rainfall. Each vine yields but two bottles of wine; thus the flavors are concentrated and the varietal character intensified.

All white wine fermentations are conducted entirely in barrels in underground cellars, designed after a typical French cave, requiring no air-conditioning to keep it cool.

As vintage succeeded vintage, Chalone learned that winemaking is a natural process that needs intelligent and sensitive guidance.

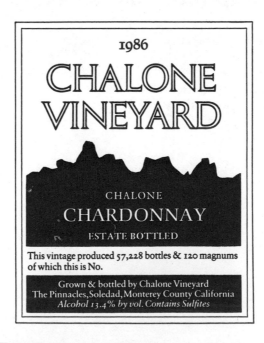

1986

## CHALONE VINEYARD

CHALONE
CHARDONNAY
ESTATE BOTTLED

This vintage produced 57,228 bottles & 120 magnums of which this is No.

Grown & bottled by Chalone Vineyard
The Pinnacles, Soledad, Monterey County California
Alcohol 13.4% by vol. Contains Sulfites

# Poached Salmon with Wine

*Preparation Time: 45 Minutes*
*Pre-heat oven to 400°*
*Serves 4 to 6*

**5-7 lbs. fresh whole salmon**
**1 tablespoon sweet butter**
**6 sprigs of fresh dill weed**
**1 lemon, sliced**
**1 bottle Chalone Chardonnay**

Clean salmon thoroughly and remove scales. Place in lightly buttered pan, arranging half of the sliced lemon and dill inside fish. Pour half the bottle of Chardonnay over fish and dot with remaining butter. Arrange several slices of lemon and dill on outside of salmon.

Cover and bake for approximately 30 minutes or until cooked to taste.

Enjoy the remainder of the Chardonnay while you wait for the fish to cook.

# CHATEAU JULIEN

8940 Carmel Valley Road
Carmel Valley, CA 93922
(408)624-2600
Tour and tasting room

CAREFULLY ORCHESTRATED CELLARING and bottle aging are instrumental parts of the Chateau Julien story. The philosophy of quality rather than quantity is stressed.

The Chateau is a delightful place to stop for a visit. Set against a backdrop of the steeply rugged Carmel Valley hills; the winery is elegantly French in style, with a distinctive California character.

Château Julien

Monterey County
Private Reserve Chardonnay
Cobblestone Vineyard

1984  PRODUCED & BOTTLED BY CHATEAU JULIEN
CARMEL CALIFORNIA B.W. 5101
ALCOHOL 13.3% BY VOLUME

# Stuffed Trout with Asparagus

*Preparation Time: 35 Minutes*
*Pre-heat oven to 350°*
*Serves 4*

6 celery stalks, finely chopped
2 cups small mushrooms, finely chopped
½ cup blanched almonds, finely chopped
2 cups canned baby clams, chopped
   Pinch tarragon
   Pinch sweet basil
4 cloves garlic, finely chopped
8 strips medium cooked bacon, chopped
4 boned trout
8 tablespoons butter
2 tablespoons reserved bacon drippings
6 tablespoons flour
1 cup clam juice
1 cup Sauvignon Blanc
1½ lbs. fresh asparagus

In a medium-sized bowl mix together chopped celery, mushrooms and almonds. Fold in clams, tarragon, basil, garlic and chopped bacon. Stuff trout with the mixture and seal fish with small skewers or toothpicks.

In an 8 × 14-inch glass baking dish place 4 tablespoons butter. Put dish in preheated 350° oven until butter is melted. Remove pan from oven and gently place the stuffed trout in the baking dish. Cover dish with aluminum foil with one corner folded back slightly. Bake for 20 to 25 minutes.

While trout is baking, place 4 tablespoons butter in medium-sized frying pan with the bacon drippings. Heat to slightly bubbling. Stir in flour and continue to stir while thickening. Lower heat. Slowly stir in clam juice and Sauvignon Blanc. Add more liquid if sauce is too thick.

Steam asparagus until tender. When trout is cooked, place it and the asparagus on a platter. Pour sauce over both. Serve.

# JEKEL VINEYARD

40155 Walnut Ave.
Greenfield, CA 93927
(408)674-5522
Tour and tasting room

JEKEL VINEYARD IS a family-owned vineyard and winery. The vineyard was planted in 1972 on 140 acres of rocky loam, just west of Greenfield.

The winery produced its first wines in 1978. Their wines have been recognized for their consistent quality by the many awards they win each year.

# Seafood Sausages

*Preparation Time: 45 Minutes (note elapsed time)*
*Makes 20 sausages*

½ lb. fresh small bay scallops
½ lb. ling cod, or other rock fish, fresh or smoked
½ lb. shrimp, peeled
½ lb. crab meat
½ lb. salmon, fresh or smoked
 6 eggs
 6 carrots diced
 8 shallots minced
 1 stalk celery chopped fine
 1 pepper, red or green, chopped
 6 oyster or shiitake mushrooms minced
 6 oz. Jekel Chardonnay
20 natural sausage casings

Grind the seafood in a food processor. Sauté the shallots, carrots, celery and pepper until soft. Blend the cooked vegetables and seafood mixture with the eggs, wine and mushrooms.

Stuff the mixture into the natural sausage casing. Sausages should set for 4 or more hours before poaching.

# Sauce

1 quart fish or clam stock
8 oz. Jekel Chardonnay
1 pint cream

Combine fish stock and wine to poach the sausages for 10 minutes over medium heat. Remove sausages and add cream.

Pour sauce over sausages and serve.

# J.LOHR WINERY

1000 Lenzen Ave.
San Jose, CA 95126
(408)288-5057
Open daily for tours and tasting

J.LOHR WINERY was bonded in 1974 on the site of the former Falstaff and Fredricksberg breweries, near downtown San Jose.

The friendly tasting room staff is available to guide you through a tasting of their Monterey County wines and take you on an educational tour of the winery.

Private tours, tastings and dinners are available by special arrangement.

# Chicken Breasts with Apple/Chardonnay Cream

*Preparation Time: 45 Minutes*
*Serves 2*

**2 chicken breasts**
**2 shallots, chopped**
**2 golden delicous apples peeled and sliced (⅛")**
**½ cup J. Lohr Chardonnay**
**½ cup chicken broth**
**2 tablespoons butter**
**½ cup cream**

Bone, skin and halve chicken breasts. Sauté in 1 tablespoon butter until cooked through. Keep warm.

Sauté apples and shallots in 1 tablespoon butter. Add chicken broth and Chardonnay. Bring to boil. When apples are tender, reduce heat and add cream.

Spoon over chicken.

# LA REINA WINERY

P.O. Box 1344
Carmel, CA 93921
(408)373-3294

THE BOUTIQUE-STYLE La Reina Winery was founded by Charles and Sandra Chrietzberg in 1984 in the small town of Gonzales in southern Monterey County.

Limiting production to Chardonnay only, the small winery quickly developed a following for its hand-crafted "Queen of Chardonnays."

While the winery cannot accommodate quests, you will find this enticing wine in area restaurants and retail stores.

La Reina

1 9 8 6

MONTEREY COUNTY

CHARDONNAY

PRODUCED AND BOTTLED BY LA REINA, SAN MARTIN, CA
ALCOHOL 12.8% BY VOLUME   CONTAINS SULFITES

# Sole La Reina

*Preparation Time: 20 Minutes*
*Serves 2*

**6 oz. La Reina Chardonnay**
**Two 6 oz. fillets of sole**
**8 oz. fish broth**
**¼ cup chopped shallots**
**2 fresh tomatoes, peeled and sliced**
**6 parsley sprigs**
**1½ teaspoon lemon juice**
**1½ teaspoon butter or margarine**

Combine Chardonnay and fish broth in a saucepan. Bring to a boil, adding shallots, parsley and lemon juice. Turn temperature down to a simmer. Place sole, folded in half, into pan and cover for 6 minutes.

Remove sole. Turn temperature back to high, allowing stock to reduce by half. Add butter or margarine, constantly stirring until it is completely blended. Add fresh tomatoes. Let simmer one minute before pouring over sole.

# Fish Broth

**1 lb. fish bones**
**½ gallon water**
**1 onion**
**2 carrots**
**2 celery stalks**
**3 bay leaves**
**1 whole lemon**
**1 teaspoon mixed pickling spice**
**1 cup La Reina Chardonnay**

Put all ingredients into a pot. Bring to a boil. Turn off and let cool. Strain through cheesecloth.

# Monkfish with Pasta & Mussels

*Preparation Time: 30 Minutes*
*Serves Four*

1½ lb. monkfish fillet
12 oz. cooked vermicelli
20-24 mussels
 ½ cup flour
 2 tablespoons oil
 2 shallots, chopped fine
 ⅔ cup La Reina Chardonnay
 1 tablespoon tomato puree
 1 tablespoon fresh basil, chopped
 9 oz. unsalted butter
 8 oz. snow peas
 2 cloves garlic, chopped
 6 oz. mushrooms, sliced
 4 oz. spinach, blanched, drained and roughly chopped
 2 oz. parmesan cheese, shredded
 6 oz. whipping cream
    Salt and pepper to taste

Cut the fish into 32 finger-shaped slices. Season and dust with flour. Sauté the monkfish in hot oil in a heavy skillet, turning once. When the fish is half cooked (2-3 minutes) add shallots, tomato puree and white wine. Cover and set aside.

Steam the mussels in a saucepan until they open. Remove from their shells and trim off the "beards". Set aside.

Gently heat the butter, garlic and mushrooms in a wide shallow saucepan. Add the spinach, pasta and cream. Turn the heat up high to reduce the cream and stir. Add half the parmesan and mussels.

Heat the snow peas in salted water so they remain crisp.

Mound the pasta mixture in the center of four hot plates. Sprinkle the rest of the parmesan on top. Surround each dome of pasta with 8 pieces of monkfish like the spokes of a wheel. Spoon wine sauce over fish and place a snow pea between each piece of fish.

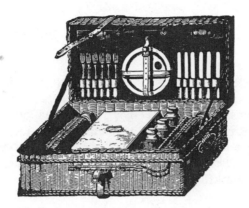

# Chardonnay Wine Mousse

*Preparation Time: 15 Minutes (note refrigeration time)*
*Serves 6*

**8 oz. La Reina Chardonnay**
   **Juice of 2 lemons**
   **Juice of 2 oranges**
**6 oz. sugar**
**6 eggs**
**¼ oz. gelatin powder**
**1 pint whipping cream**
   **Red grapes for garnish**

Place the wine and sugar in a saucepan with the lemon and orange juice and bring to a boil.

Separate the eggs, placing the yolks in a stainless steel bowl. When the wine mixture boils, pour it over the egg yolks, stirring slightly. Add the gelatin and stir. Strain the mixture to cool.

Whip the cream and fold into the cooled mixture. Pour into white wine glasses and set in the refrigerator for 1 hour.

Separate grapes into clusters of 3, dipping them into egg whites and then sugar. Place on top of the mousse for garnish.

# MIRASSOU VINEYARDS

3000 Aborn Road
San Jose, CA 95135
(408)274-4000
Open daily for tour and tasting

A MERICA'S OLDEST WINEMAKING family, Mirassou is in its fifth generation of family ownership. Pioneers in Monterey County viticulture, Mirassou Vineyards enjoy a fine reputation.

The 1983 Brut Champagne, Monterey, has captured four medals since its Spring release. A dry, well-balanced champagne, it is a blend of 56% Pinot Noir, 28% Chardonnay and 16% Pinot Blanc. This is an elegant, complex sparkling wine.

*Mirassou*

1986
Monterey County

Chardonnay

PRODUCED AND BOTTLED BY
MIRASSOU VINEYARDS, SAN JOSE, CALIFORNIA
ALCOHOL 12.5% BY VOLUME, 750 ML

# Veal Venus
### *(Loin of Veal with Sun-dried Tomatoes, Mushrooms and Garlic)*

*Preparation Time: 45 Minutes*
*Pre-heat oven to 375°*
*Serves 10-12*

**4 pounds boneless veal loin, well trimmed and tied**
**5 tablespoons olive oil**
**1½ teaspoons salt**
**1 teaspoon black pepper**
**4 garlic cloves**
**6 ounces sun-dried tomatoes packed in oil**
**4 tablespoons unsalted butter**
**4 shallots**
**2 pounds fresh mushrooms**
**1 bunch watercress**

Combine 3 tablespoons oil, 1 teaspoon salt, ½ teaspoon pepper, 2 cloves of garlic and 2 ounces sun-dried tomatoes in a food procesor or blender, and puree to a paste. Rub this mixture onto all sides of the veal loin.

Heat a large heavy sauté pan and add 2 tablespoons each of olive oil and butter. Add veal loins and sear on all sides over high heat to seal in juices. Transfer meat to a baking pan and bake in a 375° oven for approximately 25-30 minutes, until juices run light pink when meat is pricked with a fork. Remove veal from oven, cover with foil and allow to rest in a warm place for 15 minutes before carving.

While the meat is cooking, chop the shallots and mushrooms and sauté in the remaining 2 tablespoons butter. Mince 2 cloves of garlic and 4 ounces sun-dried tomatoes in a food processor. Stir into mushrooms, along with ½ teaspoon each, salt and black pepper.

To serve, remove veal strings, thinly slice veal loin and top each serving with a spoonful of mushroom mixture. Garnish with a sprig of watercress.

Serve with Mirassou Brut Champagne.

# Medallions of Veal with Pistachio Butter Sauce

*Preparation Time: One Hour*
*Pre-heat oven to 350°*
*Serves 8*

2 tablespoons unsalted butter
One 4 lb. boneless veal loin, trimmed and tied
  Salt and pepper to taste

Season veal with salt and pepper and brown in a heavy roasting pan with butter for 5 minutes. Place in a 350° oven for 30 minutes. Baste with butter several times during roasting.

Remove the meat from the oven, cover with foil and allow to rest for 15 minutes before slicing.

# Pistachio Butter Sauce

*Yield: 1½ cups*

¼ cup shallots, finely chopped
½ cup Mirassou White Burgundy
¼ cup white wine vinegar
½ cup water
¼ teaspoon salt and pepper
 8 oz. unsalted butter, cut into 16 pieces
 1 clove garlic, peeled and mashed
½ cup toasted pistachios, chopped

In a small, heavy saucepan combine the shallots, wine, vinegar, water, salt and pepper. Bring to a boil. Reduce heat and simmer until the mixture is reduced to 2 tablespoons.

Over low heat, whisk butter, one piece at a time. Whisk in the garlic and pistachios.

Slice veal into ¼ inch thick medallions and serve two per person with pistachio butter sauce spooned over the top. Serve with Mirassou Brut Reserve Champagne or White Burgundy.

# Tortellini and Prawns with Basil Vinaigrette

*Preparation Time: 40 Minutes*
*Serves 8*

1 lb. green tortellini, cooked al dente
1 lb. cooked prawns, shelled and deveined
4 cups crookneck squash or yellow zucchini thinly sliced
1 small red onion, thinly sliced and separated into rings

## Basil Vinaigrette

*Yields 2 cups*

1 cup fresh basil leaves
3 large garlic cloves, peeled
½ cup walnuts, toasted
¼ cup Parmesan cheese, grated
¼ cup red wine vinegar
½ teaspoon dry mustard
½ teaspoon salt
¼ teaspoon freshly ground black pepper
½ cup olive oil
½ cup vegetable oil

Puree all ingredients except oils in food processor or blender. With motor running, slowly add oils and process until well blended.

To assemble, combine tortellini, prawns, squash and onion rings in a large bowl. Toss with dressing and refrigerate until serving time.

Serve with Mirassou Chardonnay.

# MONTEREY PENINSULA WINERY

786 Wave Street
Monterey, CA 93940
(408)372-4949
Tasting Room

MONTEREY PENINSULA WINERY produces hand-tended wines of character. As winemakers, they believe that wine is grown in the vineyard and that they are the stewards of nature while the wine is in their cellar.

The 1985 Chardonnay represents the second consecutive vintage from Sleepy Hollow. It is one of the northernmost vineyards in the Monterey appellation and less than 15 miles from Monterey Bay. The cooling ocean breezes insure a long, cool growing season which results in good acid structure at full ripeness.

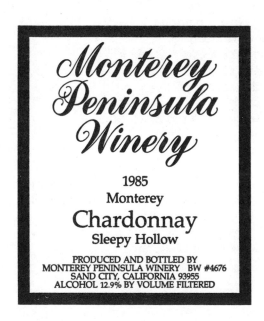

*Monterey Peninsula Winery*

1985
Monterey
Chardonnay
Sleepy Hollow

PRODUCED AND BOTTLED BY
MONTEREY PENINSULA WINERY   BW #4676
SAND CITY, CALIFORNIA 93955
ALCOHOL 12.9% BY VOLUME FILTERED

# Marinated Shrimp

*Preparation Time: 15 Minutes*
*Serves 6*

**36 medium to large shrimp**
    **Crab boil (pre-packaged at supermarket)**

# Marinade

 **1 large egg yolk**
 **¾ cup olive oil**
 **¾ cup peanut oil**
 **¾ cup red wine vinegar**
 **1 tablespoon shallots chopped**
 **3 tablespoons parsley chopped**
 **3 tablespoons chives chopped**

Devein and peel the shrimp. Boil with 3 tablespoons crab boil in the water. Remove from the heat when they turn pink. Cool in water.

Whisk the egg yolk, oils, vinegar, and mustard. Add the shallots, parsley and chives.

Drain the shrimp and put them in a serving bowl. Pour marinade over the shrimp and refrigerate for at least 2 hours, turning several times.

Enjoy with a bottle of Monterey Peninsula Chardonnay.

# THE MONTEREY VINEYARD

800 South Alta Street
Gonzales, CA 93926
(408)675-2316
Open daily for tours and tastings

THE MONTEREY VINEYARD is located outside the town of Gonzales, 25 miles inland from Monterey Bay.

The Spanish-Mexican architecture emphasizes the heritage of northern California, and the stained glass windows in the winery illustrate the different grape varieties.

The grounds encompass a museum-quality gallery featuring a permanent exhibition of Ansel Adams' "Story of a Winery", a Visitor Center where all wines are available to taste, as well as a beautiful picnic area.

THE
MONTEREY VINEYARD°

# Frittata with
# Spring Garden Vegetables

*Preparation Time: 1½ Hours*
*Pre-heat oven to 350°*
*Serves 12*

  **2 tablespoons butter**
**¼ cup olive oil**
**1 yellow onion, diced**
**2 garlic cloves, crushed**
**1 carrot, sliced in rounds**
**2 parsnips sliced into rounds**
**6 zucchini, sliced into rounds**
**3 crookneck squash, sliced into rounds**
**4-5 eggs**
  **2 tablespoons cream**
  **4 tablespoons milk**
  **1 tablespoon basil**
  **1 tablespoon thyme**
**½ pound Monterey Jack cheese, grated**
  **3 tablespoons Parmesan cheese**
     **Roasted red peppers**
     **Green chiles diced**

In a non-stick pan, sauté the onions in butter and olive oil until they are transparent. Remove from the pan. Sauté garlic and vegetable rounds until tender.

In a bowl combine eggs, cream, milk, spices, and cheeses.

Remove the vegetables from the heat and return the onions to the pan. Stir the egg mixture into the vegetables, blending quickly and thoroughly. Return the pan to the stove and heat (without sticking) until the frittata begins to set up, approximately 10 minutes. Transfer the pan to a pre-heated 350° oven for 1 hour, or until completely set and golden brown.

Remove the frittata from the oven; let cool before flipping it out onto a large serving platter. Garnish with diced roasted red peppers, diced green chiles, and extra parmesan cheese.

To serve, cut into pie-shapped wedges.

# PAUL MASSON VINEYARDS

P.O. Box 1852
Saratoga, CA 95070-0199
For Special Events and information
(408)741-5183

PAUL MASSON VINEYARDS, California's oldest continuous wine producing company and America's sixth largest, dates back to 1852.

In 1905, Paul Masson built a great stone winery at his mountain vineyard, with foundations deep into the hillside to maintain constant cool temperatures for aging wine. The 1906 earthquake shook loose thousands of bottles of Masson Champagne from their racks but did not destroy the winery.

In 1958, a series of summer concerts, Music at the Vineyards, was inaugurated at an outdoor amphitheater for which the imposing winery serves as a backdrop; the much-expanded series now attracts 60,000 music-lovers annually.

MONTEREY COUNTY
## CHARDONNAY
*Vintage 1985*

*This aristocrat of white wines is pleasantly crisp with a fragrant bouquet and rich complex flavors. Serve chilled. Alc. 12% by Vol.*

## PAUL MASSON®

*Cellared & Bottled by Paul Masson Vineyards, Gonzales, CA*

# Cold Veal Rolls

*Preparation Time: 1½ Hours*
*Serves 6*

12 Veal slices, pounded paper thin (3 × 5 inches) and dusted
    with flour
 3 tablespoons breadcrumbs
12 slices Virginia ham
12 leaves fresh sage (or ¼ teaspoon dried)
12 lettuce leaves
 3 tablespoons olive oil
 3 tablespoons chopped black olives
4-5 tablespoons unsalted butter
    Juice of 1 lemon
 1 cup Paul Masson Monterey County Chardonnay
    Salt and pepper to taste

Top each veal slice with Virginia ham, lettuce leaf and sage. Set aside. Mix breadcrumbs and black olives with olive oil, salt and pepper. Transfer some of the mixture to each veal slice. Roll up the meat tightly (egg roll style) and fasten with a cooking string. Refrigerate covered for 15 minutes.

Over low heat, melt the butter in a skillet, add the veal rolls and brown lightly for 3 minutes on each side. Add the lemon juice and Chardonnay and continue cooking for 5 minutes more, covered over medium heat.

Let cool in the pan. Remove the strings and refrigerate for 1 hour before serving.

# SMITH & HOOK WINERY

37700 Foothill Road
Soledad, CA 93960
(408)678-2132
Tour and Tasting Room

SMITH & HOOK perches on the eastern slope of the Santa Lucia Mountains, overlooking the Salinas Valley. The vineyard was purchased in 1973 after an eleven-year search that spanned three continents in pursuit of the right combination of soil, climate and vineyard exposure. The estate was created out of two ranches totalling 652 acres.

Efforts were made to retain the ranch's rustic feeling. The old stable now serves as the winery. The lab is in the former tack room, and offices are in the bunkhouse where ranch-hands once bedded down.

Smith & Hook produces only one wine, an estate-bottled Cabernet Sauvignon. With seven grape-producing slopes on the Smith & Hook wine estate, the winemaker is able to craft a Cabernet Sauvignon with a structure that demonstrates unusual complexity and quality.

# Cabernet Black Olive Pâté

*Preparation Time: 30 minutes*
*Serves 6*

    2 tablespoons olive oil
    1 bunch scallions
    3 garlic cloves, crushed
    2 medium sized tomatoes
    8 ounces black olives, minced
  ½ teaspoon dill weed
1½ cups Smith & Hook Cabernet

   Sauté scallions and garlic in oil until soft. Add the tomatoes, olives and dill weed. Cook on low heat, covered for 10 minutes. Pour in the Cabernet, bringing the mixture to a boil. Reduce heat and simmer for 20 minutes uncovered, until mixture reduces to the consistency of a soft pâté.

   Cook and serve with crackers and assorted breads.

# ROBERT TALBOTT WINERY

93 Tassajara Road
Carmel Valley, CA 93924
(408)375-0505
Tours by appointment only

TALBOTT WINERY IS fully committed to producing a very fine, full-bodied, complex Chardonnay. Barrel fermented and aged for nearly two years before release, Talbott offers a wine that is superb today... exquisite tomorrow.

Please look for their newest release, Logan Chardonnay. Continued quality without compromise.

## TALBOTT

### 1985
## Chardonnay
**Monterey**

PRODUCED & BOTTLED BY ROBERT TALBOTT VINEYARDS
CARMEL VALLEY, CALIFORNIA, USA
ALCOHOL 12.0% BY VOL. • CONTAINS SULFITES

# Lobster Thermidor

*Preparation Time: 30 Minutes*
*Pre-heat oven to 400°*
*Serves 6*

⅓ cup butter
½ cup sifted all-purpose flour
3 cups warm cream
2 tablespoons Talbott Chardonnay
   Pinch of cayenne pepper
¼ teaspoon dry mustard
½ lb. fresh mushrooms
¼ cup butter (to sauté mushrooms)
3 cups cooked lobster meat cut into 1-inch pieces
1½ teaspoons salt
¼ cup grated parmesan cheese, plus topping cheese
   Vegetable flowers and parsley for garnish

Melt ⅓ cup butter, add flour to make paste, and then add cream, a little at a time, stirring constantly, and cook until thick. Add the wine, pepper, mustard, sliced mushrooms, lobster meat and ¼ cup cheese, and sauté for 5 minutes. If mixture is too thick, add more cream.

Pour into medium-sized casserole. Sprinkle top thickly with additional cheese and drizzle melted butter over cheese. Bake 15 minutes at 400°, then broil for several minutes until top is brown. Garnish center of casserole with vegetable flowers and parsley.

Serve with an herb rice, vegetable medley of broccoli, carrots and cauliflower, mixed salad with honey mustard dressing and a bottle of Talbott Chardonnay.

# VENTANA VINEYARDS

2999 Monterey-Salinas Highway
Monterey, CA 93940
(408)372-7415
Tasting Room

THE VINEYARD WAS planted in the early 1970's by Doug Meador whose innovative farming methods have brought him everything from wild acclaim to disbelieving looks. However controversial they may be, they are almost always successful.

This is evident not only in the many fine wines of Ventana but also in the number of great wines from other labels bearing the vineyard designation of Ventana Vineyards.

The winery was established in 1978 with great enthusiasm for a new region, a strong belief in the land, a vision of world class wines on the horizon. It was a well founded belief, as Ventana Vineyards Winery has produced many award winning wines that are just that... world class.

MONTEREY
## SAUVIGNON BLANC
VENTANA VINEYARDS

PRODUCED AND BOTTLED BY VENTANA VINEYARDS
SOLEDAD, CALIFORNIA B.W. 4847 · ALCOHOL 13.4% BY VOLUME
PRODUCE OF U.S.A. · CONTAINS SULFITES

# Figs in Sauvignon Blanc with Vanilla Ice Cream

*Preparation time: 10 minutes (note elapsed time)*
*Serves 4*

    8 ripe figs
1½ cups Ventana Sauvignon Blanc
    1 pint whipping cream
    1 teaspoon vanilla
       Vanilla ice cream
  ½ cup almonds

Place peeled figs cut in half in a flat bowl with Sauvignon Blanc and marinade overnight (at least 4 hours). Reserve the figs and marinade.

Whip the cream with vanilla and refrigerate.

To serve, arrange figs on a plate and top with vanilla ice cream. Pour the marinade over the figs adding the whipped cream. Sprinkle with chopped almonds and serve.

# INDEX

# ABOUT THE AUTHORS

KATHLEEN DEVANNA FISH, a native of California, has lived in Monterey for the past ten years.

Her experience as owner-operator of three businesses in the travel and hospitality industry has been invaluable in coordinating the material for "Monterey's Secrets".

A gourmet cook, Kathleen is always looking for creative recipes that have style and character.

She and her husband, Robert, live on a boat in Monterey harbor.

FRED HERNANDEZ, assistant city editor of the Monterey Herald, formerly owned and operated a resort and restaurant near Yosemite.

A native San Franciscan, Fred is an accomplished cook who describes himself as cursed with a passion for fine food.

He lives with his wife, Nancy and their dog, Kinky, in Pacific Grove.

The Marketing Arm
P.O. Box 1994
Monterey, CA 93942

Please send _____ copies of Monterey's Secrets at $10.95 each.

Add $1.75 postage and handling for the first book ordered and $1.25 for each additional book.

Enclosed is my check for _____

Name _____

Address _____

City _____ State _____ Zip _____

☐ This is a gift. Send directly to:

Name _____

Address _____

City _____ State _____ Zip _____

☐ Autographed by the authors.

Autographed to _____